bake happy

100 Playful Desserts with Rainbow Layers,
Hidden Fillings, Billowy Frostings, and More

by JUDITH FERTIG

RUNNING PRESS
PHILADELPHIA · LONDON

Published by Running Press,
A Member of the Perseus Books Group

ISBN 978-0-7624-5379-5
Library of Congress Control Number: 2014952837

E-book ISBN 978-0-7624-5309-2

9 8 7 6 5 4 3 2 1
Digit on the right indicates the number of this printing

Designed by Ashley Haag
Edited by Kristen Green Wiewora
Typography: Zalea, Brandon Text, Archer, and Melbourne

Running Press Book Publishers
2300 Chestnut Street
Philadelphia, PA 19103-4371

Visit us on the web!
www.offthemenublog.com

To my family and friends, who inspired the *Bake Happy*
idea and taste-tested the many ways to express it.

Contents

ACKNOWLEDGMENTS

An Almond Keeping Cake to Kristen Green Wiewora, editor extraordinaire, who liked *Bake Happy* at the get-go.

A batch of gluten-free vegan Chitchat Bars to Lisa Ekus and Sally Ekus, my agents, who always take care of me.

A batch of Secret Filling Devil's Food Cupcakes to Jordana Tusman, a Bistro-Style Tarte Tatin to Carolyn Sobczak, and an unlimited supply of Razzle-Dazzle Eclairs to everyone at Running Press who had a hand in producing such a wonderful book. And a big, billowing cloud of Robin's Egg Blue Frosting to Ashley Haag who outdid herself with *Bake Happy*'s design.

A batch of Sea Salt Caramel to Mary Ann Duckers, Dee Barwick, Angie Stout, Dianne Hogerty, and Karen Adler for letting me bring a dessert for every occasion, even "It's Monday."

Introduction

AS A LONG-TIME FOOD WRITER AND COOKBOOK AUTHOR, I know ingredients and techniques. I know food histories and food policy. What tastes good and what doesn't. But what I always wanted to know was this: How can baking contribute to a happy life? In *Bake Happy*, I think I've come up with 100 little answers to that big question.

Colorful, flavorful home-baked treats signal celebration for big and small occasions alike, from a milestone birthday to an "I deserve this" coffee break. They make us feel good just to look at them, and even better when we taste them. And in a world of 24-hour news, fiscal cliffs, terrorist threats, economic recovery, and environmental concerns, we need all the happy we can get.

"One of the secrets of a happy life is continuous small treats."

Iris Murdoch, novelist

THE BAKE HAPPY CONCEPT

Basically, you:

START WITH A BLANK CANVAS—a cake batter, a sweet meringue, a pastry crust, a cheesecake, a custard, a butter-cream frosting, a cookie base. Of course, the base recipe has to be delicious and easy to follow. You won't be very happy if you spend hours in the kitchen and then your cake doesn't turn out. You will, however, be delighted as you learn how easy it is to stir together a delicious one-bowl cake, whip up a cloud-like meringue, pat a buttery crust into a tart pan, or make a brownie that you can marbleize like fine Florentine paper.

STIR IN A LITTLE FLAVOR AND COLOR. Vivid colors and flavors can invigorate your senses and heighten your mood. In the recipes that follow, I've incorporated natural ingredients that will amp up both visual and taste bud appeal: veggies and fruits, nuts, chocolate, coffee, spices, pumpkin and butternut squash, frozen fruit concentrates, and more.

ADD A LITTLE FUN. Each recipe has a unique or playful twist. Maybe the batter is speckled or dappled or marbled or striped. Maybe there's a secret flavored or colored filling in a cupcake that you don't see until you take a bite. Maybe it's a drizzle of ooey-gooey Warm Pear Caramel over a slice of Crackly-Top Pear Cake (page 207). Maybe it's a final sprinkle of a flavored "pixie dust": herbs, edible flowers, chopped nuts, flavored sugars or spice mixtures, or colored sprinkles made with natural colorings and egg white.

HOW DO THESE RECIPES BAKE YOU HAPPY?

Let us count the ways!

AROMA. Even before you taste a pastry, cake, or brownie, the scent of it baking in the oven can elevate your spirits. But why stop there? Extend the aromatic high by serving your dessert with Spice Syrup (page 28), Rosemary Caramel (page 24), or decadent Chocolate Ganache (page 27) or Hot Fudge Sauce (page 25).

ASSOCIATION. A favorite dessert prompts memories of happy occasions (or creates new ones), which, in turn, prompt feelings of well-being.

COLOR. Specific colors help lift the spirits. Try your own color therapy with Black and Whites in Color (page 106) and Rainbow Cake with Robin's Egg Blue Frosting (page 218). The color of a dessert plate or ramekin can also increase the perception of better flavor.

CONNECTION. When you bake, it's only natural to share your cookies or brownies or cupcakes with others. And that leads to building or strengthening relationships, another pillar of well-being. Chitchat Bars (page 109), Creativity Kickstarters (page 90), and Chai Cupcakes (page 165) help you start conversations, incubate new ideas, and find the social common denominator in any group.

CRAFT. Learning how to make something by hand, from scratch, can promote feelings of accomplishment, a cornerstone of happiness. The more you work with a piping bag for Warmed Sugar Meringues (page 69) or Razzle-Dazzle Éclairs (page 173) or roll out crusts for the Sparkly-Top Sour Cherry Pie (page 137), the better you will get at it. You'll also develop your own unique way of doing things.

FLAVOR. Pastry chefs know that a good dessert menu needs something fruity, something chocolate, and something creamy. From that base, there are lots of natural ingredients to choose from that will increase your pleasure. Desserts with juicy berries, orchard and tropical fruits, milk to dark chocolate, spices, spirits, or vanilla are especially happy treats.

MINDFULNESS. Baking, unlike food assembly or simpler cooking techniques, requires concentration. Try making Citrus and Browned Butter Madeleines with Burnt Honey Cream (page 153) for a true taste of being in the moment.

PLAYFULNESS. Unleash your inner artist. Make a sugar cookie quilt (page 97) or a chorus line of La Di Dahs (page 75). Add stripes, swirls, dots, spirals, layers, poufs, and sprinkles to desserts. Make them your own.

REINVENTION. Some desserts are best left the way they are, and some are open to reinterpretation. If Cousin Mabel's pumpkin pie is eagerly awaited each Thanksgiving, then it's not a good candidate for reinvention. But if the pie starts to taste a little ho-hum, or making it becomes boring, then try another version, such as Cinderella Pumpkin Tart with Toffee Glass Slippers (page 132) and see what happens. In desserts and in life, it's vital to continually keep things fresh and interesting.

THE *BAKE HAPPY* LANGUAGE OF FLAVOR

Does flavor have its own language? Think of sultry warm chocolate, snarky lemons, voluptuous vanilla, and luxurious caramel.

All of us have certain emotional associations we make with the taste of a food, some stemming from the flavor compounds in the food itself and others from the context in which we eat them.

The *Bake Happy* language of flavor might be different from yours, but it's a place to start the conversation.

BANANA	Calm before adventure, even if it's just a field trip for school
BLUEBERRY	Blue-skied mornings, wholesomeness
CARAMEL	Luxury
CHERRY	A perfect summer day
CHOCOLATE	Risk taking devil's food, shoulder to lean on, indulgence
COCONUT	Familiar yet exotic
COFFEE	Taking charge, revving up
HERBS	Refreshing, replenishing
LEMON	Tart, tangy, snarky, wisecracky: always interesting
MOCHA	Starting over
ORANGE	A brand-new day, a fresh start
PASSION FRUIT	The Dorothy Parker of fruits: acerbic, witty, too sharp for its own good
POMEGRANATE	Yearning for home
PUMPKIN	Thanksgiving and simple abundance
SALT	Attention grabbing: too much overpowers
SPICE	The comfort of nostalgia, lingering emotion
STRAWBERRY	Youth, summer
SWEET POTATO	Homecoming
VANILLA	Soft and voluptuous

"The craft is when I make something as meticulous and impeccable as I can. The art is when I bring an authentic version of myself—my voice and spirit—to the work."

Sandra Palmer Ciolino, quilt artist

Chapter One

BAKE HAPPY BASICS

RECENTLY, I LISTENED TO A TALK BY Dr. John Gray, the relationship expert who wrote *Men Are from Mars, Women Are From Venus*. He suggested something that would work very well for bakers: "Create pockets of time when you're not hurried to do the things you love." Brilliant!

"Do-ahead" is a great mantra for getting into the *Bake Happy* mode. My friend Lori McCabe, Philadelphian cookie baker par excellence, has shown me a thing or two about the power of do-ahead to make your life flow more smoothly. She and her husband love to entertain almost every weekend. To make it work, she plans ahead. First, she establishes her *mise en place*, taking the time to set up her workspace and portion out the ingredients before baking. In about an hour, she can have a batch of cookies made. She freezes unbaked cookies right on the baking sheet so all she has to do is take them out and bake them fresh. She starts baking in early fall for the holidays, stocking her freezer with an assortment of little treats for drop-in guests and other last-minute activities. By doing the bulk of the work in advance when she feels more relaxed, Lori is able to stave off stress and truly enjoy her time with friends and family.

This chapter is about making some dessert basics ahead of time so you, the baker, stay happy. The pockets of time required are basically 30 minutes or less, and the results will not only simplify your dessert preparation but also inspire your creativity. When you know you have Rosy Strawberry Syrup (page 29) or Coffee Pastry Cream (page 23) on hand, you will think up new ways to use them.

Flavored syrups add an extra zing of flavor and color to desserts all throughout the book, and they keep almost indefinitely in the refrigerator. Homemade fruit curds make the taste buds do a happy dance in blood orange or passion fruit or Meyer lemon—flavors you don't see at the grocery store. Sea Salt Caramel (page 24) and its lavender and rosemary variations become a necessity: to sneak by the spoonful, to use as a filling, or to warm and drizzle over just about anything.

Likewise, Homemade Colored Sprinkles (page 35) get color and flavor from the concentrated fruit juice or natural coloring added to dried egg whites and can be spooned into a pastry bag and piped in almost any shape before being left to dry. If you want to make shapes like hearts, you can do that. Or flat polka dots. Or squiggles. Or monograms, or even just "Happy Birthday."

"It's not life changes like a new house or a fancy car that make the most impact, but sometimes little things like the smell of an orange, that give the biggest happiness boost."

Gretchen Rubin, author of *The Happiness Project*

Blood Orange Curd

When blood oranges are in season from late fall through March, make this fabulous curd to fill tarts, cakes, and cookies; to slather on pound cake slices for Blood Orange Curd Bread Pudding (page 197); or to just lick by the spoonful. It turns a gorgeous pale coral that looks fabulous with dark blueberries or blackberries, pomegranate seeds, or other citrus fruits. You can freeze blood orange juice and zest in freezer bags to use later in the year. Meyer lemons, limes, and regular lemons also make delicious curds: see the variations on the next page.

MAKES ABOUT 2 CUPS (500 ML)

½   cup (113 g) unsalted butter

1½   cups (300 g) granulated sugar

1   tablespoon freshly grated blood orange zest

½   cup (125 ml) freshly squeezed blood orange juice
     (from about 4 blood oranges)

1   teaspoon freshly grated lemon zest

1   teaspoon freshly squeezed lemon juice

5   large eggs, beaten

Melt the butter in a heavy saucepan over medium-low heat. Whisk in the sugar, zests, and juices. Cook for about 5 minutes, or until the sugar has dissolved. In a small bowl, whisk the eggs. Whisk about ¼ cup (59 ml) of the hot sugar mixture into the eggs to temper them. Whisk the eggs back into the saucepan and continue cooking and whisking until the mixture has thickened, about 5 to 7 minutes, or until an instant-read thermometer registers 160°F (70°C). With a rubber spatula or wooden spoon, press the curd through a fine-mesh sieve into a container to remove any lumps. Let it cool to room temperature, then cover the surface of the curd with plastic wrap to prevent a "skin" from forming on the top. Store it in the refrigerator for up to 2 weeks.

(recipe continues)

FOR LEMON CURD, use ½ cup (125 ml) freshly squeezed lemon juice plus 1 teaspoon freshly squeezed lime juice in place of blood orange juice, 1 teaspoon freshly grated lemon zest in place of the blood orange zest, and 1 teaspoon freshly grated lime zest in place of lemon zest, then continue with the recipe.

FOR LIME CURD, use ½ cup (125 ml) freshly squeezed lime juice in place of blood orange juice, and 1 teaspoon freshly grated lime zest in place of the blood orange zest, then continue with the recipe. If you wish, add 1 drop of blue food coloring to the curd to create a lime green color.

FOR MEYER LEMON CURD, use ½ cup (125 ml) freshly squeezed Meyer lemon juice in place of the blood orange juice and 1 tablespoon freshly grated Meyer lemon zest in place of the blood orange zest, then continue with the recipe.

FOR PASSION FRUIT AND ORANGE CURD, use ¼ cup (59 ml) frozen passion fruit concentrate, thawed, and ¼ cup (40 ml) freshly squeezed orange juice in place of the blood orange juice and 1 tablespoon freshly grated orange zest in place of the blood orange zest, then continue with the recipe. (Look for packages of Goya brand frozen passion fruit juice concentrate at Hispanic markets.)

MAKE IT A MOUSSE

A homemade curd plus whipped cream equals an easy and delicious mousse, perfect for a cake or tart filling. Fold 1 cup (250 ml) of any homemade curd into 1 cup (250 ml) of whipped cream until smooth and evenly colored.

Tart Berry Curd

Tart berries like cranberries, blackberries, boysenberries, or black raspberries can also make a delicious curd but with less butter and egg. Spread this on a cake layer for a colorful and delicious filling or dollop it into meringue baskets or tart shells, topping with a final cloud of whipped cream.

○·· **MAKES 1 CUP (250 ML)** ··○

12 ounces (340 g) fresh or frozen cranberries, blackberries, boysenberries, or black raspberries

½ cup (100 g) granulated sugar, divided

¼ cup (60 ml) water

4 large egg yolks

3 tablespoons unsalted butter, cut into pieces, at room temperature

In a small saucepan, heat the cranberries, ¼ cup (50 g) of the sugar, and the water over medium heat. Cook until the berries are very soft and there are no whole pieces left, about 12 to 15 minutes, adding more water by the tablespoon if they stick to the bottom of the pan. With a rubber spatula or wooden spoon, press the mixture through a fine-mesh sieve into a medium bowl. Return the sieved mixture to the saucepan. Whisk the remaining ¼ cup (50 g) of sugar with the egg yolks in a small bowl, then whisk into the berry mixture in the saucepan and set over medium heat. Whisking constantly, add the butter a piece at a time, until the curd has thickened and registers 160°F on an instant-read thermometer. Remove from the heat and press the mixture again through a fine-mesh sieve into a container. Let it cool to room temperature, then cover the surface of the curd with plastic wrap to prevent a "skin" from forming on the top. Store the curd in the refrigerator for up to 1 week.

Pastry Cream

Over the years, I've made a lot of pastry creams. This version is my current favorite, with the infused lemon peel adding just that little bit of mmmmm and cornstarch replacing the usual flour for a light, gluten-free result. Pastry cream can be a filling for cakes, pastries, and tarts or the base of a soufflé mixture. And it's a perfect blank canvas for the nuance of flavors found in Razzle-Dazzle Éclairs (page 173) or soufflés.

MAKES 2 CUPS (500 ML)

2	cups (500 ml) whole milk
1	(2½-inch/5 to 6-cm) strip fresh lemon peel
½	cup (100 g) granulated sugar
6	large egg yolks
⅛	teaspoon fine salt
⅓	cup (40 g) cornstarch, sifted
1	teaspoon vanilla extract
3½	tablespoons unsalted butter, cut into small pieces, at room temperature

Place the milk, lemon peel, and ¼ cup (50 g) of the sugar in a saucepan over medium-high heat. Bring to a boil. Remove the pan from the heat. Scoop out the lemon peel and discard it. Whisk the egg yolks in a medium bowl with the remaining ¼ cup (50 g) of sugar and the salt. Whisk in the cornstarch until the mixture is smooth. Pour ½ cup (125 ml) of the hot milk mixture into the egg mixture and whisk until smooth. Pour the egg mixture back into the saucepan and place it over medium-low heat. Cook, whisking constantly, until the mixture begins to thicken and registers 170°F on an instant-read thermometer, about 6 to 8 minutes. Remove the pan from the heat and whisk in the vanilla. Scoop the pastry cream into a bowl, cover the top with plastic wrap, and let it cool to room temperature. Transfer the bowl to the refrigerator and chill until ready to use. Pastry cream will keep for up to 1 week in the refrigerator.

FOR LAVENDER, Lemon, Orange, Lime, or Blood Orange Pastry Cream, simply substitute 2 teaspoons of culinary-grade dried lavender buds or freshly grated citrus zest for the lemon peel and combine with the milk in a saucepan over medium-high heat. When bubbles form around the perimeter of the pan, cover the pan and remove it from the heat. Let the milk mixture steep for 30 minutes, then strain it through a fine-mesh sieve and continue with the recipe.

FOR LAVENDER-LEMON PASTRY CREAM, substitute 1 teaspoon culinary-grade dried lavender buds and 1 teaspoon freshly grated lemon zest for the lemon peel and combine with the milk in a saucepan over medium-high heat. When bubbles form around the perimeter of the pan, cover

and remove from the heat. Let the milk mixture steep for 30 minutes, then strain it through a fine-mesh sieve and continue with the recipe.

FOR COFFEE PASTRY CREAM, use 1 teaspoon instant espresso powder or instant coffee in place of the lemon peel and proceed with the recipe.

FOR VERY EASY VARIATIONS, whisk 2 tablespoons to ¼ cup (60 ml) of a liqueur or a homemade syrup, such as Grand Marnier, Limoncello, Spice Syrup (page 28), or Passion Fruit Syrup (page 31), into warm, freshly made pastry cream until smooth. Avoid purple or dark-colored liqueurs as they can turn the pastry cream an unpleasant color.

SO HAPPY TOGETHER

Meringues + Pastry Cream

Meringues and pastry cream naturally go together, as you use egg whites for one, egg yolks for the other. So after making pastry cream (6 yolks), scurry on over to Warmed Sugar Meringues (6 whites) (page 69). You'll feel that same sense of completion that you get from tying up loose ends but in a much more delicious way. Then put them together for really wonderful Marvelous Merveilleux (page 71).

Sea Salt Caramel

What's amazing is how such simple ingredients combine to make something so luxurious and versatile. When this caramel is warm, you can pour it like a sauce and drizzle it on cookies (see Browned Butter Cookies on page 100) or brownies; when it's chilled, you can spread it on a cake layer. Artisan chocolatier Christopher Elbow makes toothsome truffles with this caramel. If you infuse the cream with lavender or rosemary first, you take the caramel from spooning to swooning. As designer Marc Jacobs says, "I think there is something about luxury—it's not something people need, but it's what they want. It really pulls at their hearts." That's the language that caramel speaks.

MAKES ABOUT 2²/₃ CUPS (650 ML)

2   cups (400 g) granulated sugar
1   cup (250 ml) water
12   tablespoons (170 g) unsalted butter
1   cup (250 ml) heavy whipping cream
1   teaspoon fleur de sel or fine sea salt

Combine the sugar and water in a heavy-bottomed 3-quart saucepan over medium-high heat. Clamp a candy thermometer to the inside of the pan. As the sugar begins to melt, stir it with a whisk or a long-handled wooden spoon. When the syrup comes to a boil, stop stirring and remove the spoon. When bubbles that rise to the top get bigger and wider, the sugar is ready to turn color, usually in about 10 to 12 minutes after it first begins to boil. Have oven mitts and the remaining ingredients ready and be vigilant. The sugar mixture will turn pale tan, then get darker. Remove the caramel from the heat when it is dark amber and the candy thermometer registers 300°F (150°C).

With oven mitts on to protect your hands from splatters, whisk in the butter until it has melted. The caramel will foam up, then subside. Wait for 30 seconds and then whisk in the cream and salt until the caramel is smooth. Remove the pan from the heat and let the caramel cool for several minutes, then serve it right away or pour it into a glass jar. The sauce will keep in an airtight container in the refrigerator for up to 3 months. To reheat the caramel for later use, microwave on medium-high for 1 to 2 minutes or until warmed through.

VARIATIONS

FOR LAVENDER CARAMEL, combine ½ teaspoon culinary-grade dried lavender buds with the cream in a microwave-safe bowl. Microwave on high for 90 seconds. Cover the bowl and let the cream infuse for 30 minutes at room temperature. Strain out the lavender, then proceed with the recipe.

FOR ROSEMARY CARAMEL, add one 3-inch sprig of fresh rosemary to the cream in a microwave-safe bowl. Microwave on high for 90 seconds. Cover the bowl and let the cream infuse for 30 minutes at room temperature. Remove the rosemary, then proceed with the recipe.

Hot Fudge Sauce

If Chocolate Ganache (page 27) is a little black dress, Hot Fudge Sauce is that perfect pair of jeans. It can go with anything—ice cream, baked pears, pound cake, meringues, Peanut Butter Bread Pudding (page 199), custard, or as a dipping sauce for peanut butter cookies. And this one is so roasty-toasty-fudgy good that you will want to eat it on everything. Store it in a glass jar in the refrigerator, where it will keep for weeks. Hot Fudge Sauce can be doubled or tripled easily, so it makes a great gift from your kitchen. The corn syrup helps the sauce stay fluid.

MAKES ABOUT 2 CUPS (500 ML)

⅔ cup (130 g) granulated sugar

½ cup (60 g) unsweetened cocoa powder

2 tablespoons instant espresso powder

¼ teaspoon fine salt

¾ cup (175 ml) heavy whipping cream

½ cup (125 ml) light corn syrup

2 tablespoons unsalted butter

1 teaspoon vanilla extract

Combine the sugar, cocoa powder, espresso powder, salt, cream, and corn syrup in a medium saucepan over medium-high heat. Bring the mixture to a boil and cook for 4 minutes, whisking constantly. Remove the pan from the heat and whisk in the butter and vanilla until smooth. Store the syrup in a tightly sealed glass jar in the refrigerator, where it will keep for weeks.

"I like to think that I'm really tough on the outside, with a caramel-sweet center."

Reese Witherspoon, actor

Chocolate Ganache

Chocolate ganache is simplicity itself to make. You just heat the cream, let the chocolate melt a little bit in it, and then whisk it all together until dark and shiny. Used warm, ganache makes a wonderful shiny coating for a cake or a lovely sauce. Once thickened and at room temperature, it makes a great filling for Marvelous Merveilleux (page 71), Macaronettes (page 148), or Coconut Lover's Cupcakes (page 156).

MAKES ABOUT 2 CUPS (500 ML)

1   cup (250 ml) heavy whipping cream

8   ounces (222 g) semisweet chocolate chips

Bring the cream to a simmer in a saucepan over medium-high heat. Add the chocolate chips, without stirring, and remove the pan from the heat. Let the pan sit for 3 minutes, then whisk the cream until the chocolate has melted and the ganache is a glossy dark brown. Use right away as a sauce or topping, or cover the pan and refrigerate it for at least 30 minutes to use the ganache as a filling or frosting.

VARIATIONS

FOR BOURBON CHOCOLATE GANACHE, stir 3 tablespoons of bourbon into the warm ganache until smooth.

FOR MOCHA GANACHE, whisk 1 teaspoon of instant espresso powder into the cream and proceed with the recipe.

FOR VENEZUELAN SPICED CHOCOLATE GANACHE, whisk ¼ teaspoon of ground chipotle, ½ teaspoon of ground cinnamon, and 1 teaspoon of vanilla extract into the cream and proceed with the recipe.

FOR VEGAN CHOCOLATE GANACHE, use coconut milk coffee creamer in place of cream and dairy-free dark chocolate chips in place of semisweet chocolate chips and proceed with the recipe.

Spice Syrup

Craft cocktail makers know all about the power of aromatizing a drink right before serving. Bakers, too, know the heady appeal of a dessert warm from the oven. So drizzling a warmed spice syrup over the custard and filo pastry known as Bougatsa (page 118) or baked apples makes sensual sense, as does adding a little bit to Pastry Cream (page 22) or whipped cream for a wonderful, nuanced flavor. Toasting the whole spices in a skillet brings the volatile oils to the surface for more aroma and flavor. The syrup is also delicious on custard, ice cream, pancakes and waffles, or pound cake.

MAKES ABOUT 1 CUP (250 ML)

2 tablespoons mixed whole spices, such as allspice, cloves, star anise, coriander seeds, and Szechuan peppercorns

½ cup (125 ml) boiling water

¾ cup (160 g) granulated sugar

Scatter the whole spices in a single layer in a small skillet over medium heat and toast, gently shaking the pan until you can just start to smell their aroma, about 2 minutes. Do not let them smoke. Pour the boiling water into a small bowl and add the spices. Cover the bowl and let the mixture steep for at least 2 hours.

Strain the spice water through a fine-mesh sieve into a microwave-safe bowl and stir in the sugar. (Let the whole spices dry on a paper towel after straining them out, then place them in a plastic bag and store them for two to three more uses.) Microwave on high for 2 minutes or until the sugar has dissolved and the spice syrup is aromatic. Use the syrup right away or store it in a small tightly sealed jar in the refrigerator for up to 3 months.

Rosy Strawberry Syrup

Once you've tasted the tiny strawberries known as fraises des bois, *you're spoiled for life. Adapted from a recipe by the late Lee Bailey, this aromatic syrup adds* frais de bois *flavor to fresh strawberries in Strawberry Shortcut Cake with Basil Whipped Cream (page 23), and Strawberry Birthday Cake (page 221). This recipe also works with raspberries, black raspberries, and blackberries. It looks like a lot of rosewater in this recipe, but it's just enough.*

MAKES 1½ CUPS (375 ML)

8   ounces (250 g) strawberries, hulled and sliced

½   cup (100 g) granulated or raw sugar

1   cup (250 ml) water

1   tablespoon rosewater

½   teaspoon freshly squeezed lemon juice

Combine the strawberries, sugar, and water in a medium saucepan over medium-high heat and bring the mixture to a boil. Reduce the heat to medium-low and simmer for 20 minutes. Remove the pan from the heat and stir in the rosewater. Strain the syrup through a fine-mesh sieve into a bowl; discard the solids. Stir in the lemon juice. Let the syrup cool, then use it right away or store it in a covered jar in the refrigerator for up to 1 week.

SO HAPPY TOGETHER

Red Berries + Rosewater

You might think that adding rosewater to fruit will result in an experience like "being pressed to your auntie's perfumed cleavage," as Niki Segnit so memorably writes in *The Flavor Thesaurus: Pairings, Recipes and Ideas for the Creative Cook*. But you would be wrong. To strawberries, raspberries, and red currants, rosewater adds "an unfathomable background note," Segnit explains. To me, the combined flavor is reminiscent of sun-warmed berries, picked ripe and eaten on the spot.

Fresh Herb Syrup

For an aromatic, sweet herb finish, toss fresh berries in this pale green syrup or add a little bit to Pastry Cream (page 22) or whipped cream for an understated flavor surprise. Fresh Herb Syrup is totally delicious in the Berry Patch Tart (page 129), but it would also be good brushed on the cut sides of Strawberry Shortcut Cake (page 231) before piling on the strawberries.

○········· MAKES ABOUT 1 CUP (250 ML) ·········○

1 cup (200 g) granulated sugar

¾ cup (175 ml) water

½ cup (60 g) packed fresh aromatic herb leaves, such as basil, orange mint, spearmint, or lemon balm, coarsely chopped

In a large, microwave-safe glass measuring cup, combine the sugar, water, and herbs. Microwave on high until the sugar dissolves, about 3 to 4 minutes. Let the mixture steep for 20 to 30 minutes at room temperature, then strain it through a fine-mesh sieve into a medium bowl; discard the solids. Let the syrup cool and use it right away or store it in a covered glass jar in the refrigerator for up to 2 weeks.

"Spices are essential in that they bring excitement to a dish. Without spices, a dish is sometimes lacking in soul."

Eric Ripert, chef of Le Bernardin Restaurant in New York

Passion Fruit Syrup

For a tart, wake-up-your-taste-buds finish, toss fresh berries with this pale pink syrup and spoon the mixture over Miniature Pavlovas (page 72) or Gooey Butter Bars (page 146). It's a great way to make Pastry Cream (page 22) really interesting and your éclairs (page 173) more glamorous. Fresh passion fruits are not readily available in the Midwest (and the pulp will include seeds), so I use the Goya brand of packaged frozen fruit juice concentrate that I find in markets that carry lots of Hispanic products.

MAKES ABOUT 1 CUP (250 ML)

1   cup (200 g) granulated or raw sugar

½   cup (125 ml) fresh passion fruit pulp or frozen passion fruit juice concentrate, thawed

¼   cup freshly squeezed orange juice

In a large, microwave-safe glass measuring cup, combine the sugar, passion fruit pulp or concentrate, and orange juice. Microwave on high until the sugar dissolves, about 3 to 4 minutes. Let the mixture steep for 20 to 30 minutes at room temperature, then strain it through a fine-mesh sieve into a medium bowl; discard the solids. Let the syrup cool and use it right away or store it in a covered glass jar in the refrigerator for up to 2 weeks.

SO HAPPY TOGETHER

Passion Fruit + Orange

Passion fruit is the wild and crazy one, while orange says, "Tone it down a bit." Orange helps take the edge off passion fruit and make it more dessert-friendly.

Orange-Cardamom Syrup

Drizzled over Citrus-Glazed Sweet Potato Bundt Cake (page 216), fresh cut citrus fruit, or Citrus-Cardamom Twinkies (page 158), this heady syrup dazzles.

MAKES ABOUT 1 CUP (250 ML)

1   cup (200 g) granulated or raw sugar
     Zest and juice of 1 orange
½   cup (125 ml) water
1   teaspoon cardamom seeds or ½ teaspoon ground
     cardamom

In a large, microwave-safe glass measuring cup, combine the sugar, orange zest and juice, water, and cardamom. Microwave on high until the sugar dissolves, about 3 to 4 minutes. Let the mixture steep for 20 to 30 minutes at room temperature, then strain it through a fine-mesh sieve into a medium bowl; discard the solids. Let the syrup cool and use it right away or store it in a covered glass jar in the refrigerator for up to 2 weeks.

SO HAPPY TOGETHER

Orange + Cardamom

Cardamom, a member of the ginger family, is native to Pakistan, Bhutan, Nepal, and India. When paired with orange, this aromatic green spice takes on slightly mysterious and edgy characteristics.

Plate Paint

I wanted a thick, viscous, translucent "paint" made with fruit juice in order to create dots, squiggles, zigzags, or spirals to plated desserts. So, I went into the kitchen and played around a little bit. The happy result is this Plate Paint, which is edible, colorful, easy, vegan, gluten-free, and very shapeable at room temperature. Use any type of colorful bottled fruit juice (cherry, cranberry, kiwi, mango, papaya, or pomegranate). You can also try frozen Goya "fruta" concentrates (bright yellow passion fruit, deep pink guava, or blackberry).

MAKES ABOUT ⅔ CUP (150 ML)

1 tablespoon cornstarch
1 cup (250 ml) colorful bottled fruit juice or frozen fruit juice concentrate, thawed

Spoon the cornstarch into a small jar with a lid. Add the fruit juice, secure the lid, and shake to blend. Pour the juice mixture into a small saucepan over medium-high heat, and whisk it constantly until the juice begins to boil and turns from a lighter opaque color to a darker, more transparent one. Keep whisking until the "paint" begins to thicken slightly. Remove the pan from the heat and set it aside to cool to room temperature. Use the paint right away or store it in a jar with a lid in the refrigerator for up to 1 week. Let the paint come to room temperature before using.

PAINT YOUR PLATE

Add a playful or colorful dimension to a slice of pie, a meringue, a brownie, or any other dessert by embellishing the plate with fun, edible color.

To make a dot, let about ½ teaspoon of Plate Paint drip off a small spoon, held just above the plate.

To make a squiggle, spoon 1 tablespoon of Plate Paint at the 12 o'clock point on the plate. Use the back of a teaspoon to press down into the paint and zigzag down to the 6 o'clock point on the plate.

To make a zigzag, pour the paint into a plastic squeeze bottle and secure the top. Make sure the opening is at least ¼ inch in diameter. Turn the bottle upside down and squeeze a zigzag onto each plate.

To make a spiral, pour the paint into a plastic squeeze bottle and secure the top. Make sure the opening is at least ¼ inch in diameter. Turn the bottle upside down and squeeze a spiral, starting at the center of the plate and moving outward.

To make a spider web, make a spiral on the plate. Using a toothpick or a cake tester, start at the center and drag it through the paint in "rays" going out toward the rim of the plate. Repeat until you have a spider web shape.

Homemade Colored Sprinkles

You can create your own custom colored sprinkles with this recipe, inspired by pastry chef Stella Parks in Louisville, Kentucky, who blogs at Brave Tart. When I first made these, I used powdered egg white instead of fresh for keeping quality, then stirred in strongly brewed hibiscus tea to make pale lavender sprinkles for baby shower cupcakes. I was hooked. Using store-bought sprinkles now feels like coloring inside the lines. You can flavor and color these however you wish for a special occasion or simply to celebrate your favorite color combinations. Use your sprinkles for Confetti Cookies (page 94) or one-of-a-kind cake toppers. You'll need a pastry tip to pipe the mixture in parallel rows of tiny lines; I found #134 and #89 tips and disposable piping bags at Michael's and other craft and cake-decorating stores. Just pipe out the mixture into tiny lines on baking sheets, and let them dry at room temperature for about 24 hours. When they're dry all the way through, cut them into sprinkles and use them right away or store them indefinitely in an airtight container in the pantry. You can also make larger designs using other types of piping tips. Just let them dry completely before using them to decorate cakes and cupcakes.

MAKES ABOUT 1 CUP (250 ML)

1 cup (120 g) confectioners' sugar, sifted
½ teaspoon fine salt
2 teaspoons dried egg whites
2½ tablespoons water
1 teaspoon vanilla extract or other flavored extract
Food coloring or natural flavorings (see Variations, page 36)

Line two large baking sheets with parchment paper and set them aside. In a medium bowl, whisk together the confectioners' sugar and salt. In a small bowl, stir the dried egg whites and water together until well blended. Whisk the egg white mixture into the confectioners' sugar. Whisk in the vanilla and drops of food coloring until the desired color is reached.

Fit a pastry bag with a #134 or #89 tip. Spoon the sprinkle mixture into the pastry bag. Pipe tiny lines in parallel rows on the prepared baking sheets. Let the sprinkle batter dry at room temperature for 24 hours, then use a chef's knife to cut it into small sprinkles. Store the sprinkles in an airtight container in the pantry for up to 6 months.

(recipe continues)

FOR HIBISCUS (PALE LAVENDER), use 1 tablespoon strongly brewed hibiscus tea in place of the vanilla extract and food coloring.

FOR FRESH MINT (PALE GREEN), use 2 to 3 drops of green food coloring and 1 teaspoon of peppermint extract in place of the vanilla extract.

FOR SNOW CONE RASPBERRY (TURQUOISE), use turquoise food coloring and 2 teaspoons of raspberry extract in place of the vanilla extract.

FOR SAFFRON (PALE GOLD), steep ¼ teaspoon saffron threads in 1 tablespoon of boiling water for 15 minutes. Strain the liquid through a fine-mesh sieve, then use it in place of the food coloring and vanilla extract.

FOR CREAMSICLE (PALE ORANGE), use 2 to 3 drops of orange food coloring and 2 teaspoons of orange extract in place of the vanilla extract.

PIXIE DUST

A little pixie dust sprinkled on a finished dessert adds that last bit of color and flavor. Think outside the colored sprinkle box for new options.

At an Indian or Pakistani grocery, look for Mumbai Mix or other sugar-coated fennel, coriander, and sesame seed mixtures: the breath mints of the sub-continent. Mumbai Mix looks wonderful on Chai Cupcakes (page 165) and fits their flavor profile.

Crush old-fashioned peppermint sticks between sheets of parchment paper, using a meat mallet or a rolling pin. Sprinkle them on chocolate confections or on Marvelous Merveilleux (page 71).

Crush cookies or graham crackers, then dust them over mellow pumpkin and squash desserts, such as Sweet Dumpling Tartlets with Maple Custard (page 121).

For a really aromatic sprinkle, try Sweet Orange Mint Gremolata (page 90) on Twinkies (page 158) or frosted cupcakes.

To make your own colored sugar, simply put about ½ cup (100 g) raw organic sugar (it works best) in a small bowl. Use gel food coloring and put a dab on the end of a toothpick. Work the gel coloring into the sugar until you achieve the color you want. Store the colored sugar indefinitely in a tightly sealed plastic bag in the pantry.

Toffee Glass Slippers

Shiny, hard caramel can be broken into shards to dress up all kinds of desserts. If you like, customize this brittle with fresh chopped rosemary, dried lavender buds, dried rose petals, finely chopped nuts, toasted green pumpkin seeds, or cocoa nibs sprinkled over the warm candy.

MAKES ABOUT 2 CUPS (500 ML) CANDY BRITTLE PIECES

Canola oil for the pan

¾ cup (160 g) granulated sugar

¼ cup (60 ml) water

½ teaspoon coarse kosher or sea salt

Line a small baking sheet with aluminum foil and lightly brush with oil. Clamp a candy thermometer to the inside of a medium saucepan.

Stir the sugar and water together in the saucepan over medium-high heat. Let the mixture cook without stirring for about 8 to 10 minutes or until it turns a dark amber, at around 300°F (150°C) on the candy thermometer. Carefully pour the candy onto the prepared pan, spreading evenly, then sprinkle it with salt. Let the candy cool completely, then break it into shards and use it right away or store it in an airtight container at room temperature for up to 1 week.

VARIATIONS

FOR ROSEMARY, Lavender, or Rosy Glass Slippers, sprinkle 2 tablespoons of very finely chopped rosemary leaves, dried lavender buds, or dried rosebuds with the coarse kosher or sea salt over the warm candy.

FOR PUMPKIN SEED GLASS SLIPPERS, sprinkle ½ cup (125 ml) of toasted, salted pumpkin seeds on the prepared baking sheet, then pour the warm candy over them.

FOR NUTTY TOFFEE GLASS SLIPPERS, sprinkle ½ cup (125 ml) of toasted, chopped pecans, almonds, or hazelnuts on the prepared baking sheet, then pour the warm toffee over them.

FOR COCOA NIB GLASS SLIPPERS, sprinkle 2 tablespoons of finely chopped cocoa nibs over the warm candy with the salt.

Cinderella Pastry

This recipe makes enough pastry (the same pastry as for Cinderella Pumpkin Tart with Toffee Glass Slippers on page 132) for two tarts, so wrap and freeze the rest for up to 3 months.

MAKES ENOUGH FOR 2 (8-INCH/20-CM) TARTS

1½ cups (225 g) unbleached all-purpose flour

½ cup (60 g) confectioners' sugar, sifted

½ cup plus ½ tablespoon (125g) unsalted butter, chilled and cut into small pieces

3 large egg yolks

1 tablespoon freshly squeezed lemon juice

Combine the flour, confectioners' sugar, and butter in a food processor and pulse to blend until the mixture resembles fine crumbs. Add the egg yolks, lemon juice, and 2 tablespoons of water and pulse just until the dough comes together into a ball. Divide the dough in half and form each half into a disc. If not using right away, double-wrap and freeze the discs for later use, for up to 3 months.

Sweet Almond Pastry

With a slight hint of almond, this sweet pastry rolls out easily for a tart or a crostata.

1 cup (227 g) unsalted butter, chilled

2¼ cups (280 g) unbleached all-purpose flour, sifted

¼ teaspoon baking powder

½ teaspoon fine salt

⅓ cup (67 g) granulated sugar

½ teaspoon almond extract

3 tablespoons ice water

Place the butter, flour, baking powder, salt, and sugar in the bowl of a food processor fitted with a steel blade or in a medium bowl. Pulse the food processor or use a pastry blender to cut the butter into the dry ingredients until the mixture resembles pea-size crumbs. Sprinkle the mixture with the almond extract and water, then pulse again or mix with a fork until the dough comes together to a ball. If not using right away, wrap the dough in a disc well and refrigerate for a day or freeze for up to 3 months.

Chapter Two

FRUIT

THE SIMPLEST DISHES TO HELP YOU BAKE HAPPY START with the honest, straightforward, homey qualities of fruit. These desserts can follow the seasons, be as local as possible, and deliver big flavor without a lot of fuss. With easy enhancements like port wine, honey, lemon zest, vanilla bean, and spices, baked fruit aromatizes your kitchen first, then pleases your eye and your palate. And oh, the colors!

With fruit, you get the complete Roy G. Biv of the rainbow: red in Honey Baked Apples (page 44) or Skillet Cranberries (page 59); orange in Pandan Leaf Papaya with Sweet Coconut Cream (page 53) or Vanilla Baked Apricots (page 58); yellow in Brûléed Pineapple (page 48); a hint of green in Green Tomato and Pear Mostarda (page 49); and blue-indigo-violet in Lemon-Zested Mulberry and Rhubarb Crisp (page 51) and Port-Glazed Plums (page 47).

Fruit desserts are delicious alone, but many in this chapter can also be the building blocks of more complicated desserts. For example, a slice of pound cake or a Warmed Sugar Meringue (page 69) can accompany any kind of baked fruit, topped with a drizzle of warm Sea Salt Caramel (page 24) or homemade fruit syrup (page 29) in a complementary flavor. A square of gingerbread with Vanilla Baked Apricots (page 58), a Gooey Butter Bar (page 146), or a slice of Almond Keeping Cake (page 211) with Skillet Cranberries (page 59) can all be tasty blank canvases for the colorful energy of baked fruit.

"This special feeling towards fruit, its glory and abundance, is I would say universal. . . . We respond to strawberry fields or cherry orchards with a delight that a cabbage patch or even an elegant vegetable garden cannot provoke."

Jane Grigson, British food journalist and cookbook author

Honey Baked Apples

Iconic food writer M.F.K. Fisher let the unique flavor of each apple guide her as to how to bake it. "I like to dig out the cores, sniff the flavor, and then stuff them with raw sugar or leftover jam or mincemeat, according to their messages," she wrote in Bon Appétit *in 1979. This recipe works for all kinds of apples, particularly a cherry-red variety that will hold its shape during baking, such as Jonathan, Ida Red, Northern Spy, Empire, or Rome Beauty, an heirloom apple from Rome, Ohio. Served on a rectangular white tray in a pool of honeyed sauce, these red apples look like a colorful, abstract Marimekko fabric pattern, and their cinnamon-orange fragrance will make you feel like all is well with your world. Use a paring knife to peel and core the apples, taking care not to cut all the way through to the bottom of the apple. It's easier to stir and baste with the honey if it is warmed for 10 seconds in the microwave first.*

MAKES 4 SERVINGS

Vegetable oil, for the baking dish

4   red apples, peeled a third of the way down and cored

½   cup (100 ml) clover or wildflower honey, warmed

½   teaspoon freshly grated orange zest

½   teaspoon ground cinnamon

Preheat the oven to 375°F (190°C). Oil an 8-inch (20-cm) square or 9-inch (23-cm) round baking dish. Arrange the apples in the baking dish so that they are not touching. In a small bowl, stir together ¼ cup (60 ml) of the honey, the orange zest, and the cinnamon until well blended. Spoon 1 tablespoon of the honey mixture into the cavity of each apple.

Bake the apples for 15 minutes, then baste them with the sauce that collects in the baking dish. Return the dish to the oven. Baste every 15 minutes until the apples have baked for 45 minutes. Then, baste with the remaining ¼ cup of warmed honey and bake for 15 more minutes or until the apples are soft. Remove the dish from the oven and let the apples rest for 10 minutes; serve warm.

Buttery Apple and Black Walnut Charlotte

Aromatic and delicious, this homey dessert is just the antidote for cold weather. Black walnuts grow wild throughout the Midwest, where you can buy shelled black walnuts at the grocery store. You can also find black walnuts online through www.hammonsproducts.com. Like all nuts with volatile oils, black walnuts keep better when frozen; thaw before using in a recipe. Make this recipe gluten-free by using gluten-free bread. Golden Delicious apples caramelize and soften more quickly than other apple varieties at higher heat.

MAKES 8 SERVINGS

6 to 8 slices good-quality sandwich bread, crusts removed

¾ cup (170 g) unsalted butter, melted

¼ cup (60 ml) apple juice or apple cider

1½ pounds (680 g) Golden Delicious apples, peeled, cored, and thinly sliced

½ cup (100 g) granulated sugar

1 teaspoon instant tapioca

½ cup (50 g) black walnuts, chopped

Preheat the oven to 400°F (200°C). Dip or brush both sides of each bread slice with the melted butter, then line the bottom and sides of a 1-quart (1-L) soufflé dish, metal mixing bowl, or charlotte mold with the buttered bread slices, cutting them to fit. Save the remaining buttered bread slices for the top. Set the prepared dish aside.

Place the apple juice, apples, sugar, and tapioca in a medium saucepan over medium-high heat. Cook, stirring, until the apples have softened, about 15 minutes. Stir in the black walnuts. Spoon the apple filling into the bread-lined dish. Arrange the remaining bread slices on top to make a lid.

Bake for 20 minutes, then reduce the oven temperature to 350°F (180°C) and bake for 20 minutes more, or until the charlotte is browned on top and bubbling. Remove the charlotte from the oven and let it cool in the dish until just warm. Spoon the charlotte onto individual plates right from the dish, or, if you like, loosen the sides of the charlotte from the dish with a table knife, invert it onto a serving platter, and cut it into slices. Serve with ice cream, if desired.

SO HAPPY TOGETHER

Apple + Black Walnut

If there ever was a taste marriage made in heaven, this is it. I'm not terribly fond of black walnuts by themselves, but paired with apple, *whoa boy*. Fragrant and slightly tart-sweet apples meet musky, aromatic black walnuts and flavor sparks fly. If you can't find black walnuts in your area or don't want to order them online, make this charlotte with pecans instead. It will still be delicious.

Port-Glazed Plums

Plums and port, a fortified wine with a deep "purple" flavor, makes for a delicious and sophisticated pairing. When plums are in season, serve this gluten-free, vegan dish with a dollop of vegan coconut milk yogurt and a garnish of edible lavender or purple garden flowers—ones that you grew or that you know to be edible and untreated by chemicals. The shiny, deep purple plums look wonderful on yellow plates, the color opposite of purple on the color wheel.

MAKES 2 SERVINGS

Unsalted butter, for the baking dish

8 ounces (220 g) purple plums (about 2 large)

⅓ cup (75 ml) Port wine

2 tablespoons granulated sugar

Vegan coconut milk yogurt, for garnish

Edible lavender or purple garden flowers, such as cleome, lavender, phlox, or chive blossoms, for garnish

Preheat the oven to 350°F (180°C). Butter an 8-inch (20-cm) square baking dish.

Cut the plums in half and pit them. Place the plums cut-side down in the prepared baking dish. Drizzle each plum with a quarter of the port, then sprinkle each with a quarter of the sugar. Cover and bake for 30 to 35 minutes, or until the plums are tender when pierced with a fork. Serve immediately or let the plums cool to room temperature. To serve, transfer two plum halves to a dessert plate. Drizzle each half with a little of the cooking liquid. Add a dollop of coconut milk yogurt and garnish with a purple flower.

SO HAPPY TOGETHER

Plum + Port

Fresh plums send mixed messages—sharp, tart skin and mild, sweet flesh. But bake any variety of purple plums with a little port, a fortified red wine from Oporto in Spain, and you have something greater than the sum of its parts: sophisticated, voluptuous, silky, dark purple deliciousness.

Brûléed Pineapple

This is so simple and yet so good, especially in the winter months when cabin fever strikes. At Picholine in New York City, brûléed pineapple is served with sweet coconut rice, a passion fruit–flavored cake, and a tropical fruit sauce. Any leftovers are delicious for breakfast.

MAKES 6 SERVINGS

Baking spray

1 (3-pound/1.36-kg) pineapple, peeled and cored, flesh cut into spears

1 tablespoon unsalted butter

⅓ cup (63 g) packed light brown sugar

1 tablespoon water

½ teaspoon ground cinnamon

2 tablespoons dark rum

Preheat the oven to 500°F (260°C). Line a 9-inch (23-cm) baking dish with aluminum foil and spray it with baking spray.

Arrange the pineapple spears in a single layer in the prepared baking dish. In a small saucepan over medium heat, melt the butter and stir in the brown sugar, water, cinnamon, and rum. Cook, stirring, until the sauce comes together, about 3 minutes. Pour the sauce over the pineapple.

Bake until the pineapple has developed a crackly, sugary coating, about 7 to 10 minutes. If you like, serve this warm with Passion Fruit and Orange Curd (page 20), frozen yogurt, or ice cream.

Green Tomato and Pear Mostarda

Lovers of spiced pumpkin butter and mincemeat won't be able to leave this Italian dish alone. There are all kinds of imported fruity/spicy mostardas, and they're very pricey. When I was working on a kitchen garden story about Cody Hogan, the chef-behind-the-scenes for Lidia Bastianich's television program, he made this version for us. He served the aromatic mostarda in a sage green and burnt umber hand-thrown baking dish, and it almost looked too pretty to eat. But we did. Spoon this on toasted pound cake slices, ice cream, or Gooey Butter Bars (page 146) for a sharp-tasting complement. Says Hogan, "Mostarda can personalize and dress up so many foods—from dessert to Thanksgiving turkey—I can hardly imagine living without it." The skins on pear, tomato, and apple bake to a tender and colorful finish.

MAKES ABOUT 4 CUPS (1 L)

½ cup (43 g) yellow mustard seeds

1½ cups (375 ml) water

1½ cups (375 ml) apple cider vinegar or white wine vinegar

½ cup (125 ml) honey

½ cup (100 g) granulated sugar

½ teaspoon crushed red pepper flakes

1 teaspoon fine salt

3 firm red pears

2 firm medium green (unripe) tomatoes or 1 Granny Smith apple

Combine the mustard seeds, water, vinegar, honey, sugar, red pepper flakes, and salt in a small heavy saucepan and bring the mixture to a gentle simmer over low heat. Cook, stirring often, until the mustard seeds are plump and tender, about 45 minutes. If they look like they're beginning to dry out, add water as needed to keep them barely submerged.

Preheat the oven to 400°F (200°C). Slice the pears into 1-inch/2.5-cm-thick slices and remove the stems and cores. In a 13 x 9-inch (33 x 23-cm) baking dish, arrange the slices in a single layer. Cut the green tomatoes into ¾-inch dice (if using an apple, stem, core, and dice it). Sprinkle them on and around the pear slices. Pour the mustard syrup over all. Transfer the dish to the oven and cook until the pears are tender and lightly browned, about 30 to 45 minutes. If the fruit looks like it will dry out or scorch, add a little water. Remove the baking dish from the oven. Serve the mostarda warm, at room temperature, or cold. Cover and keep any leftovers in the refrigerator for up to 2 weeks.

Lemon-Zested Mulberry and Rhubarb Crisp

Mulberries ripen in mid- to late June and are very perishable, which is why you don't see them at grocery stores. I used to pick the purple, blackberry-like berries around the parking lots of my dentist and the local library, identifying the scrubby trees from their three differently shaped leaves. My children were appalled that I would do something so weird, which was part of the subversive appeal to me. Now I see mulberries at farmers' markets, too, in the Kansas City area. Wild mulberries are sweet and sort of bland, which makes them the perfect wallflower sidekick for the more assertive rhubarb. The lemon zest in the buttery streusel topping makes the match work. If you can't find mulberries, use blackberries. If any of this crisp makes it past dessert, it's delicious for breakfast.

MAKES 8 SERVINGS

½ cup (113 g) unsalted butter, plus more for the baking dish

10 ounces (288 g) mulberries or blackberries, rinsed and patted dry

14 ounces (400 g) rhubarb, cut into 1-inch pieces

2 cups (500 g) granulated sugar, divided

1 tablespoon instant tapioca

Zest and juice of 1 lemon, divided

1 cup (125 g) unbleached all-purpose flour

Preheat the oven to 375°F (190°C). Butter a 1-quart (1-L) baking dish.

In a large bowl, mix together the mulberries, rhubarb, 1 cup (250 g) of the sugar, the tapioca, and the lemon juice.

Dump the fruit mixture into the prepared baking dish. In a small bowl, mix together the remaining 1 cup (250 g) of sugar, the flour, and the lemon zest. Using your fingers, rub the ½ cup (113 g) of butter into the flour mixture to form large crumbs. Sprinkle these large crumbs on top of the fruit and bake for 35 minutes until bubbling. Serve the crisp warm or at room temperature, spooned into bowls or onto plates.

"One of the delights of life is eating with friends; second to that is talking about eating. And, for an unsurpassed double whammy, there is talking about eating while you are eating with friends."

Laurie Colwin, novelist and cookbook author

Brandied Pear and Fig Pudding with Brown Sugar Pecans

When carolers warble, "Oh, bring us a figgy pudding," they must mean this one. Baked in an orange-scented custard, this dessert is quick enough to make for a weeknight—and delicious the next morning for breakfast. Use the leftover egg whites to make meringues (see Chapter Three, page 63).

MAKES 6 SERVINGS

BROWN SUGAR PECANS

2	tablespoons unsalted butter, melted, plus more for the baking dish
½	cup (99 g) pecan pieces
1	tablespoon packed dark brown sugar
⅛	teaspoon fine salt

BRANDIED PEAR AND FIG PUDDING

¼	cup (60 ml) brandy or Grand Marnier
¼	cup (60 ml) water
½	cup (100 g) granulated or raw sugar
4	ounces (120 grams) dried figs, about 12
1	tablespoon freshly squeezed lemon juice
3	Bosc pears, peeled and cut in half
4	large egg yolks
1¾	cup (425 ml) half-and-half
2	teaspoons freshly grated orange zest

Preheat the oven to 325°F (160°C). Butter the inside of 9-inch (23-cm) square baking dish.

For the Brown Sugar Pecans, arrange the pecan pieces in a single layer on a small baking sheet and toast them in the oven for 10 minutes until fragrant. Transfer the pecans to a small bowl and toss them with the melted butter, brown sugar, and salt. Set aside.

For the Brandied Pear and Fig Pudding, stir together the brandy, water, and sugar in a medium microwave-safe bowl. Add the figs and stir to blend. Cover the bowl and microwave on high for 1 minute. Stir the mixture again, then microwave on high for another 2 minutes until the sugar has dissolved and the dried figs have partially softened. Add the lemon juice and pear halves to the bowl and gently toss to coat the pears in the liquid. Let the pears soak in the liquid for 10 minutes at room temperature.

Meanwhile, bring a kettle of water to a boil.

In a medium mixing bowl, whisk the egg yolks with the half-and-half and orange zest until the mixture is thick and pale yellow, about 2 minutes. Remove the pears and figs from their bowl with a slotted spoon and arrange them in the prepared baking dish. Pour the remaining brandied liquid into the egg mixture and whisk to blend, then pour the custard over the fruit. Set the baking dish in a larger, high-sided pan, and pour the boiling water into the larger pan until it comes halfway up the sides of the baking dish.

Bake for 30 minutes or until the fruit is tender and the custard has set. Sprinkle the Brown Sugar Pecans on top and serve hot or cold.

Pandan Leaf Papaya with Sweet Coconut Cream

Similar to a bay leaf, the tropical pandan leaf helps flavor and perfume fresh papaya as it bakes. You can find pandan leaves fresh or frozen at Asian or Middle Eastern markets. You simply tie a knot in the middle of the pandan leaf and put it in the center of each papaya half. Not only does it flavor the papaya, but it also scents your home. If you've ever wondered what to do with a papaya other than eating it fresh, then this is for you. You can also make this vegan, gluten-free recipe with mangoes.

MAKES 4 SERVINGS

2   small or Solo papayas, cut in half lengthwise and seeded

½   cup (125 ml) canned coconut milk

2   tablespoons packed light brown sugar or date sugar

4   small pandan leaves, fresh or frozen and thawed, tied in the middle, or 4 fresh bay or kaffir lime leaves

Preheat the oven to 375°F (190°C). Line a 13 x 9-inch (33 x 23-cm) baking dish with parchment paper and set it aside.

Place the papayas, cut-side up, in the prepared baking dish. In a small bowl, whisk together the coconut milk and brown sugar. Brush the cut surfaces of each papaya with the mixture, and reserve the rest. Place a tied pandan leaf in the cavity of each papaya.

Bake for 15 minutes, then brush the papayas with some of the remaining coconut milk mixture. Return the baking dish to the oven, bake the papayas for another 15 minutes, and brush them again with the remaining coconut milk mixture. Return the baking dish once more to the oven and bake for another 5 minutes or until the papayas are soft and browned at the edges but still retain their shape. To serve, remove the pandan leaves and serve each papaya half in a shallow bowl.

Rum and Brown Sugar Banana Fool

What grows together goes together in this dish of tropical fruit and the fruits of the sugar cane. I much prefer baked bananas to fresh ones, as baking concentrates their flavor. And, of course, anything caramelized—or made with rum—just has to be better! A "fool" is an old English dessert made with puréed or mashed cooked fruit and fluffy cream.

MAKES 6 SERVINGS

2   very ripe bananas
2   tablespoons white, dark, or spiced rum
2   tablespoons packed light brown sugar
1   cup (250 ml) heavy whipping cream or crème fraîche
     Freshly grated nutmeg, for garnish
     Freshly grated chocolate, for garnish

Preheat the oven to 425°F (220°C). Line a 9-inch (23-cm) baking square dish with foil. Place six martini glasses in the freezer to chill.

Arrange the bananas in the prepared baking dish. Drizzle them with the rum and sprinkle the sugar over top.

Bake for 15 to 20 minutes or until the bananas are caramelized and soft. Remove the baking dish from the oven and let the bananas cool, then mash them in the baking dish.

Whip the cream in a medium bowl until stiff peaks form and fold the whipped cream into the mashed, caramelized bananas using a wooden spoon. (If you are using crème fraîche, simply fold it into the bananas as is, no need to whip it.)

Divide the fool among the six chilled martini glasses. Top each portion with some grated nutmeg and grated chocolate and serve.

SO HAPPY TOGETHER

Rum + Bananas

Bananas are so benign that they need a little adventure, which is where the rum comes in. Distilled from tropical sugar cane, rum's piratical reputation helps mild bananas live a little.

Rustic Cherry Batter Pudding

A traditional French clafoutis involves dark, sweet cherries baked in an eggy batter. In this twist on the classic, which is based on a recipe by Anne Willan, award-winning doyenne of French cuisine, a batter pudding made with sour cherries is baked in a cabbage leaf-lined dish. Although the cabbage leaves give the batter a surprisingly light and sweetly perfumed flavor, the rustic look of the dish is what counts here. If you don't feel adventurous, simply bake the batter pudding without the cabbage leaves. It still tastes delicious. Batter pudding is best enjoyed the day it is made.

MAKES 8 SERVINGS

¾   cup (85 g) unbleached all-purpose flour

½   teaspoon fine salt

1   cup (200 g) granulated or raw sugar

4   large eggs

1   cup (250 ml) half-and-half
    Unsalted butter, for the pan

8   to 10 large, perfect green cabbage leaves

2   tablespoons kirsch or 1 teaspoon almond extract

4   cups (680 g) fresh, frozen and thawed, or canned and
    drained pitted sour cherries

Sift the flour into a large bowl. Stir in the salt and sugar, and make a well in the center. Add the eggs and ½ cup (125 ml) of the half-and-half and whisk until the batter is thick and well combined. Whisk in the remaining ½ cup (125 ml) of half-and-half until the batter is smooth and pourable. Cover the bowl and set it aside at room temperature for about 30 minutes.

Preheat the oven to 400°F (200°C). Butter a large,

14-inch (35-cm) oval baking or gratin dish and set it aside on a large baking sheet.

Bring a large pot of water to a boil over high heat. Drop in the cabbage leaves and blanch them for 2 minutes, then immediately drain the pot and transfer the leaves to a paper towel–lined plate to drain. Pat the leaves gently to blot and flatten the leaves. With a paring knife, trim away any tough stems.

Line the prepared baking pan with the blanched cabbage leaves, curling the leaves over the rim of the dish, like a frill. Trim the leaves, if necessary, to create a pleasing appearance.

Stir the kirsch and the cherries into the batter. Pour the batter into cabbage-lined pan.

Bake for 35 to 45 minutes, or until the cabbage leaves have lightly browned and a cake tester inserted in the middle of the pudding comes out clean. The filling will puff up but then deflate when the dish comes out of the oven. Scoop the pudding out of the baking dish and serve warm or at room temperature. This is best enjoyed the same day it is made.

Vanilla Baked Apricots

Fresh apricots always look promising at the market, but for most of the year they don't always deliver on flavor—unless, of course, you're in Italy, where almost everything tastes better. So if you want good apricot flavor at home in the off-season, you have to use dried apricots. These syrupy apricots are delicious simply served warm in a bowl with honeyed Greek yogurt. They're also great as a topping for Gooey Butter Bars (page 146), Cane Syrup Gingerbread (page 208), or Luscious Cream Cheese Pound Cake (page 217), and make sure to save any leftover syrup to drizzle over pancakes or waffles. If you can't find the smaller dried Mediterranean apricots, substitute them with an equal weight of the larger California ones.

MAKES 4 SERVINGS

1	(7-ounce/198-g) package dried Mediterranean apricots
1	cup (250 ml) water
¼	cup (50 g) granulated sugar
1	vanilla bean
2	teaspoons freshly squeezed lemon juice

Preheat the oven to 350°F (180°C).

In a covered baking dish, mix together the apricots, water, and sugar. With a paring knife, split the vanilla bean lengthwise, scrape the seeds into the baking dish, and then drop in the vanilla bean halves.

Bake the apricots, covered, for 45 minutes or until they have softened and plumped. Remove the dish from the oven and stir in the lemon juice. Serve the apricots right away or keep them in the refrigerator, covered, for up to 1 week.

Skillet Cranberries

President John Adams was fond of cranberries baked in a skillet, and for good reason. They get a little crispy and caramelized, and their tart flavor and deep cranberry color are intensified. Serve these with Warmed Sugar Meringues (page 69), pound cake, Almond Keeping Cake (page 211), or Gooey Butter Bars (page 146).

MAKES 6 SERVINGS

1 (12-ounce/340-g) bag fresh or frozen and thawed cranberries

¾ cup (160 g) granulated sugar

¼ cup (59 ml) kirsch, amaretto, or brandy (optional)

Preheat the oven to 350°F (180°C).

In a cast iron or other ovenproof skillet, toss together the cranberries and sugar.

Cover the skillet with a lid or aluminum foil and place it in the oven. Bake the cranberries for 45 minutes or until they have softened and caramelized. Remove skillet from the oven, take off the lid, and stir in the kirsch. Serve them right away or let the cranberries cool to a thick, sauce-like consistency. Keep them in the refrigerator, covered, for up to 1 week.

Lemon-Berry Whirligigs

Founded in 1853, Elsah Landing is a Mississippi River port on the Illinois side of Mark Twain country, a landscape where limestone caves, berry patches, and "whirligigs" (windmills) are still common features on rolling prairie farms. In the 1970s, Elsah Landing Restaurant founders Helen Crafton and Dorothy Lindgren developed quite a following for their delicious homemade breads and desserts like this one, which I came across in the 1981 Elsah Landing Restaurant Cookbook. *In my adaptation below, a biscuit-like dough is spread with sweet lemon butter, rolled up jelly-roll style, then sliced and baked on a bed of berry filling. Although Elsah Landing Restaurant is a now closed, this dessert has become a fond memory.*

◦ ⋯⋯⋯⋯⋯⋯⋯⋯ **MAKES 8 TO 10 SERVINGS** ⋯⋯⋯⋯⋯⋯⋯⋯ ◦

Unsalted butter, for the baking dish

LEMON-BERRY FILLING

- ⅔ cup (130 g) granulated sugar
- 2 tablespoons quick-cooking tapioca
- ½ teaspoon ground cinnamon
- ¼ teaspoon fine salt
- ¼ teaspoon freshly grated nutmeg
- 1 cup (250 ml) hot water
- 12 ounces (340 g) fresh or frozen berries, such as raspberries, blueberries, black raspberries, or blackberries, or a mixture (thawed if frozen)

WHIRLIGIGS

- 1 cup (125 g) unbleached all-purpose flour
- 2 teaspoons baking powder
- ½ teaspoon fine salt
- 3 tablespoons vegetable shortening
- 1 large egg, beaten
- 2 tablespoons heavy whipping cream or half-and-half, plus more for serving
- ¼ cup (50 g) granulated sugar
- 2 tablespoons unsalted butter, melted
- 1 teaspoon freshly grated lemon zest

Preheat the oven to 400°F (200°C). Butter a 10-inch (22.5-cm) round baking or soufflé dish and set it aside.

For the Lemon-Berry Filling, mix together the sugar, tapioca, cinnamon, salt, and nutmeg in a medium saucepan. Whisk in the hot water, place the pan over medium-high heat, and bring the mixture to a boil. Cook, whisking constantly, until the mixture thickens and the tapioca has softened, about 5 minutes. Sprinkle the berries in the bottom of the prepared baking dish and pour the hot mixture over them. Set the dish aside.

For the Whirligigs, in a medium mixing bowl, sift together the flour, baking powder, and salt. Cut in the shortening with a pastry blender or two knives. Add the egg and cream to the flour mixture and stir with a fork to make a stiff dough.

Turn the dough out onto a lightly floured surface and roll it into a 6 x 12-inch (15 x 30-cm) rectangle. In a small bowl, mix together the sugar, melted butter, and lemon zest. Brush the lemon butter over the surface of the dough. Roll the dough up like a jelly roll, starting with a 12-inch (30-cm) side. Cut the roll crosswise into 12 slices and place the slices on top of the berries in the baking dish.

Bake until the whirligigs are golden brown, about 15 minutes. Remove the baking dish from the oven and let it rest for 5 minutes, then spoon the dessert into serving dishes and pour a little cream over each portion.

Chapter Three

MERINGUES
and
SOUFFLÉS

MERINGUES, THOSE LIGHT-AS-AIR CONFECTIONS MADE WITH
sugar and whipped egg white, are enjoying a resurgence in popularity. Naturally gluten-free and very low in fat, meringues strike a fine balance between prudence and indulgence, practicality and whimsy. You can enjoy one meringue with hardly a dent to your diet. Or you can go to the other extreme and have a bakery box full of Marvelous Merveilleux (page 71) slathered with whipped cream and covered in shaved chocolate.

If you're a novice at meringue-making, then you'll need to know a few things before you get started. First of all, egg whites whip up the best at room temperature. Do not use egg whites in a refrigerated carton, as they won't achieve the volume you want.

There are three basic stages to meringue. Stage one involves beating the egg whites—usually with cream of tartar, salt, or lemon juice—until foamy. If you keep beating, you'll get to stage two, the soft peak stage, in which the meringue has turned white, still looks slightly foamy, and makes a droopy rounded peak when you swipe your finger through it. Stage three is the stiff peak stage, usually achieved after 5 to 7 minutes of high-speed beating. At this point the meringue will be glossy white, and when you test it with your finger, it will form a peak that looks like an ocean wave about to break.

Each of several methods for dissolving the sugar into the egg whites will produce a different kind of meringue. You can warm the sugar in the oven first for a Warmed Sugar Meringue (page 69), the classic meringue of the French patisserie, so crisp that is shatters when you take a bite. You can make a sugar syrup first for a billowy Italian meringue, delicious as a whipped topping or as Polka Dots (page 76). You can heat the egg whites and sugar together so the sugar melts for a Swiss Meringue, the favorite base for bakery cake buttercream frosting. Or, for a sturdier meringue, you can use confectioners' sugar in place of all or part of the granulated sugar.

When a meringue meets a fruit purée or a pastry cream, you have a soufflé, which sounds much more difficult to make than it really it is. Tiny soufflés are especially delightful. Bake them in small ramekins or teacups for a charming sweet nothing at the end of a meal.

Making meringues will also leave you with leftover egg yolks, which you can cover and store in the refrigerator for a few days. But why not use them at the same time, so you don't have refrigerator clutter? Shuffle back to Chapter One and use the egg yolks to make Pastry Cream (page 22), or flip ahead to Chapter Seven and make Scented Custard (page 181) or Persimmon Flans with Honeyed Whipped Cream (page 187).

SO HAPPY TOGETHER

Egg Whites + Sugar

Egg whites and sugar, mixed together using different techniques and then baked, can produce meringues with unique qualities. It seems like magic, but it's just baking science.

SUGAR	METHOD	RESULT
Granulated	Whipped with egg white	Chewy, marshmallowy
Granulated	Sugar warmed in oven first	Glossy, brittle
Granulated and confectioners'	Whipped with egg white	Solid, sturdy
Granulated	Hot sugar syrup	Billowy, soft, stable for many uses
Granulated	Sugar and egg whites heated together	Ethereal for buttercream frosting

Swiss Meringue

Swiss meringue is delicious as a bright, glossy, billowy topping for tartlets and Luscious Lemon Meringue Pie (page 139), or as a frosting for chocolate or coconut cakes, similar to Seven-Minute Frosting (page 156). Making this type of meringue is also a first step in making Swiss Meringue Buttercream Frosting (page 205), the preferred frosting for special occasion and wedding cakes. This makes enough to generously top a 9-inch (23-cm) pie or frost a 9-inch (23-cm) two-layer cake

MAKES ABOUT 4 CUPS (1 L)

1¾ cups (370 g) granulated sugar

6 large egg whites

¼ teaspoon cream of tartar

In a small saucepan or in the bottom of a double boiler, bring about 2 inches of water to a simmer over medium heat. Place a medium metal mixing bowl or the top of the double boiler over the water, but do not let the water touch the bottom of the bowl. Add the sugar, egg whites, and cream of tartar to the bowl and whisk well to blend. Using a handheld electric mixer, beat the mixture over the heat on medium speed until it begins to turn white, then increase the speed to high and beat until the meringue is glossy and will hold a stiff peak, about 7 minutes total. Immediately remove the bowl from over the simmering water so the meringue stays smooth. Use the meringue right away or cover the bowl and store it at room temperature for up to 24 hours.

Loop-de-Loop Italian Meringue

This type of meringue has a light and airy texture perfect for adding loop-de-loops, curlicues, and snowy white flour-ishes to all kinds of desserts. To make it, you simply beat a heavy sugar syrup into stiffly beaten egg whites, then use it right away to frost a two-layer 9-inch (23-cm) cake or 24 cupcakes or to top two lemon meringue pies. You can also cover the bowl and store it in the fridge for up to a week. Soak the saucepan in hot water to melt off any hardened syrup. This makes enough to generously top a 9-inch (23-cm) pie or frost a 9-inch (23-cm) two-layer cake.

MAKES ABOUT 4 CUPS (1 L)

½   cup (125 ml) water
1   cup (225 g) granulated sugar
4   large egg whites
¼   teaspoon cream of tartar

Clamp a candy thermometer to the inside of a heavy-bottomed saucepan, pour in the water and sugar, and heat the mixture over low heat until the sugar dissolves, about 3 minutes. Increase the heat to medium-high and bring the mixture to a boil. Cook for about 12 to 15 minutes until the mixture regis-ters 248°F (120°C) on the candy thermometer. This is the hard ball stage, or the point at which the hot mixture will form a hard ball when dropped into a glass of cold water. Immediately remove the pan from the heat.

While the sugar syrup is cooking, in the bowl of an electric mixer, beat the egg whites and cream of tartar until stiff peaks form, about 7 minutes. Set aside.

Wearing an oven mitt on the hand holding the saucepan, gradually pour the hot sugar syrup into the beaten egg whites with the electric mixer going on low speed. Increase the mixer speed to medium-high and continue beating until all the syrup is incorporated and the meringue is thick and glossy, about 4 minutes more.

Use the meringue right away or cover it and store it in the refrigerator for up to 1 week.

"The power of finding beauty in the humblest things makes home happy and life lovely."

Louisa May Alcott

Forgotten Pudding

This easy recipe is "pudding" as in the British word for dessert and "forgotten" in that you leave it to finish overnight in a cooling oven. Naturally gluten-free, this rectangle of soft meringue has a toasty top and a marshmallow-y center. Like a Pavlova, it calls out for something sharp-flavored as well as something smooth and creamy to round it out. This recipe is adapted from a recipe in Classic Home Desserts: A Treasury of Heirloom and Contemporary Recipes *by the late, great Richard Sax.*

························· MAKES 8 SERVINGS ·························

2   tablespoons unsalted butter, at room temperature, for the pan

6   large egg whites

½   teaspoon cream of tartar

½   teaspoon fine salt

1¼   cups (250 g) granulated sugar

2   teaspoons vanilla extract

2   cups (490 g) honeyed Greek yogurt, such as The Greek Gods brand

12   ounces (340 g) mixed fresh berries, such as raspberries, blueberries, and blackberries

Preheat the oven to 450°F (230°C). Line a 13 x 9-inch (33 x 23-cm) baking pan with parchment paper. Butter the parchment paper and the sides of the pan. Set aside.

In the bowl of an electric mixer, beat the egg whites, cream of tartar, and salt until soft peaks form, about 4 minutes. Add the sugar, a little at a time, then add the vanilla and beat the mixture on high speed until stiff peaks form, about 8 minutes total. Spread the meringue in an even layer in the prepared pan.

Bake the meringue for 15 minutes, then turn the oven off. Leave the pan to slowly cool and dry out for 8 hours or overnight. Serve the meringue right away or store it in the refrigerator, uncovered, for up to 10 hours.

To serve, use a paring knife to loosen the meringue from the sides of the pan, then invert the pan onto a flat surface. Cut the meringue into squares, dollop each square with honeyed yogurt, and scatter with berries. This is best enjoyed the same day it is made.

Warmed Sugar Meringues

For this type of meringue, you warm the sugar in the oven while you beat the egg whites, then incorporate the two. Warming the sugar first helps it incorporate faster into the egg whites, a technique perfected by French bakers. The resulting glossy (and gluten-free) meringues have a sugar-crisp texture, unlike commercial meringues, which can have a dusty taste of cornstarch. These shatter when you take a bite, which makes them perfect for Marvelous Merveilleux (page 71), but they are also delicious topped with just a pouf of whipped cream and a drizzle of dessert sauce. Warmed Sugar Meringues also pair well with Chocolate Ganache (page 27) and fresh fruit. The Poppyseed Meringues (see variation below) are delicious with Lemon Curd (page 20).

MAKES 16 TO 20 (4-INCH/10-CM) MERINGUES

1⅓ cups (267 g) granulated sugar

4 large egg whites

¼ teaspoon fine salt

Preheat the oven to 400°F (200°C). Fit a disposable pastry bag with a star or #8 tip; set aside. Line two large baking sheets with parchment paper.

Spread the sugar in a thin layer on one of the prepared baking sheets. Bake the sugar for 8 minutes, or until it starts to dissolve at the edges of the baking sheet, then remove the baking sheet from the oven. Reduce the oven temperature to 100°F (50°C) or as low as your oven will go.

While the sugar is warming in the oven, in the bowl of an electric mixer, beat the egg whites until soft peaks form, about 4 minutes. Once you take the sugar out of the oven, set the mixer speed to low, then carefully lift the parchment paper from the baking sheet and tip the hot sugar into the egg whites. Return the parchment paper to the baking sheet. Turn the mixer to medium speed and beat until the egg whites are thick and glossy white, about 10 minutes. Beat in the salt.

Transfer the mixture to the prepared pastry bag and pipe eight to ten (4-inch/10-cm) circles on each prepared baking sheet.

Bake the meringues for 5 to 6 hours or until they are crisp and dry. If you're baking these at a temperature higher than 100°F (50°C), check them after 4 hours. Do not let them brown. These meringues will keep for several days, uncovered, in a dry kitchen.

VARIATIONS

FOR POPPYSEED MERINGUES, fold 2 tablespoons of poppy seeds into the meringue mixture before piping.

FOR COFFEE MERINGUES, add 2 teaspoons of espresso powder or instant coffee to the egg whites with the baked sugar.

Marvelous Merveilleux

Merveilleux (loosely translated as "wonderfuls") are little meringue layer cakes frosted with whipped cream and dusted with Belgian spice cookie dust, grated chocolate, or even colored sprinkles. There may or may not be a secret filling. At Au Merveilleux de Fred in Paris or O Merveilleux in New York City's Upper East Side, you can order a trio of these meringue confections flavored with coffee and dusted with shaved white and dark chocolate and Belgian speculoos cookie dust. Writes Paris-based blogger and cookbook author David Lebovitz of his merveilleux experience: "I bought three small meringues to share with friends, and when sitting on a nearby park bench waiting for one of them to arrive, I dug into the first meringue. I don't swear on this blog so I won't share exactly what I said, but take it from me, a few expletives were uttered. Then I dug, and dug, and dug, until the once beautiful box was scraped clean, and all that remained were a few bits of chocolate and cream so well-lodged in the corners, that even my extremely persistent digging with a little spoon wouldn't release them. Then the box got tossed before the friend arrived so no one was the wiser, which goes to show how good intentions can so easily go astray."

MAKES FOUR 2-LAYER MERINGUES

2   cups (500 ml) heavy whipping cream, chilled

2   teaspoons vanilla extract

1   teaspoon espresso powder or instant coffee (optional)

8   Warmed Sugar Meringues (page 69)

5   ounces (142 g) grated dark chocolate or white chocolate, or about 12 speculoos cookies, such as Biscoff, finely crushed

In the bowl of an electric mixer, beat together the cream and vanilla until thick and billowy, about 8 minutes. (If you like, remove one-third of the whipped cream and stir in the espresso powder.) Sandwich two meringues together with vanilla- or coffee-flavored whipped cream until you have four 2-layer meringues. Using an offset spatula, frost the sides and tops of the two-layer meringues. Chill the frosted meringues, uncovered, in the refrigerator for 30 minutes.

Scatter the grated chocolate or crushed cookies on a parchment paper–lined baking sheet. Roll each frosted meringue layer "cake" in the topping until the sides are well coated.

Garnish the tops with more chocolate or cookie dust and serve on rectangular plates with forks and big napkins.

Miniature Pavlovas

This quintessential Australian dessert, named after ballerina Anna Pavlova, can be a colorful play of taste and texture. A little drop of vinegar helps the meringue stay crisp on the outside and marshmallow-y and chewy on the inside, while a sharp-tasting, creamy fruit curd adds complementary flavor and color, and fresh fruit, tossed with a flavored syrup, provides the finish. It's a beautiful presentation—until you cut it, and then it's a mess. That's why I like to make miniature nests instead of one big Pavlova, so each person has his or her own little meringue. Traditionally, Pavlovas are served with fresh passion fruit and whipped cream, but tiny fresh passion fruits can be hard to find. For this recipe I use frozen passion fruit concentrate (available at Hispanic markets) to give flavor and color to both the curd and the syrup for the blueberries. You can make the Passion Fruit and Orange Curd (page 20) and Passion Fruit Syrup (page 31) ahead of time, or mix and match other fruit curds, syrups, and berries.

○ ········· **MAKES 8 MINIATURE PAVLOVAS** ········· ○

Baking spray

PAVLOVA
5	large egg whites
⅛	teaspoon fine salt
1	cup (200 g) granulated sugar
1	tablespoon cornstarch
1	teaspoon vanilla extract
2	teaspoons distilled white vinegar
1	recipe Passion Fruit and Orange Curd or other citrus fruit curd (page 20)

PASSION FRUIT BLUEBERRIES
2	cups (300 g) fresh blueberries
½	cup (125 ml) Passion Fruit Syrup (page 31)

Preheat the oven to 250°F (120°C). Line a large baking sheet with aluminum foil and spray the foil with baking spray.

In the bowl of an electric mixer, beat the egg whites and salt until foamy, about 4 minutes. In a small bowl, stir together the sugar and cornstarch and add the mixture to the egg whites in a slow, steady stream, beating constantly. Continue to beat the egg whites on high speed until they are glossy and form stiff peaks, about 7 minutes total. Beat in the vanilla and vinegar.

Pipe or spoon the meringue into 3-inch/8-cm-diameter mounds about 2 inches (5 cm) apart on the prepared baking sheet.

Bake until the meringues are crisp and dry to the touch, about 50 minutes, then turn the oven off and let the meringues dry out in the cooling oven for 1 hour.

For the Passion Fruit Blueberries, toss the berries with the Passion Fruit Syrup in a bowl until well coated. Set aside.

To serve, set the Pavlovas on individual plates. Top each serving with Passion Fruit and Orange Curd and a spoonful of Passion Fruit Blueberries.

Midnight Stars

Crisp white meringue cookies piped in star shapes have many virtues. As varied as the stars in an evening sky, these cookies can take on any number of flavorings, from the citrus touch used here to coffee, cinnamon, hazelnut, or black walnut. They are easy to make, low in fat, and keep well in an airtight container. After a heavy meal, they're just the thing to serve with coffee, gently piled into a cobalt blue bowl. Superfine sugar can be found in the baking aisles of most major grocery stores, but you can make your own at home by simply processing granulated sugar for a minute or so in the food processor.

MAKES 5 DOZEN MERINGUES

5   large egg whites

¼   teaspoon cream of tartar

½   cup (100 g) superfine sugar

½   cup (60 g) confectioners' sugar, sifted

1   teaspoon finely grated lemon or orange zest

Preheat the oven to 200°F (100°C). Line two baking sheets with parchment paper and set them aside. Fit a pastry bag with a star tip and set it aside.

In the bowl of an electric mixer, beat the egg whites and cream of tartar until they soft peaks form, about 4 minutes. Beat in the sugars, ¼ cup at a time, until the meringue turns glossy white and forms stiff peaks, about 7 minutes total. With a rubber spatula, fold the grated citrus zest into the meringue. Quickly spoon the meringue into the prepared pastry bag. Pipe stars about 1 inch (2.5 cm) apart onto the prepared baking sheets.

Bake for 1 hour, or until the stars are dry and crisp to the touch. Remove the baking sheets from the oven and serve the meringues immediately, or store them in an airtight container at room temperature for up to 1 week.

VARIATIONS

FOR OTHER FLAVORINGS, swap out the citrus zest for 1 tablespoon of instant coffee powder, 1 teaspoon of ground cinnamon, or 1 cup (250 ml) of very finely ground toasted hazelnuts or black walnuts.

La Di Dahs

The Whimsical Candy Company, founded by Chris Kadow-Dougherty in Chicago, makes delightful apostrophe-shaped treats of white chocolate nougat swirled around sea salt caramel, then dipped in dark chocolate. They looked and tasted so fabulous that I wondered how I could come up with a baked version. And then I had that eureka moment—meringue! The combination of blank canvas almond meringue with Lavender Caramel (page 24) and dark chocolate gives you three complementary flavors in one scrumptious bite.

MAKES 32 TO 36 MERINGUES

6	large egg whites
2½	tablespoons granulated sugar
2½	cups (300 g) confectioners' sugar, sifted
¾	cup (90 g) finely ground almonds or almond meal
1	cup (175 g) semisweet chocolate chips
1	recipe Lavender Caramel (page 24)

Preheat the oven to 325°F (160°C). Line two large baking sheets with parchment paper and set them aside.

In the bowl of an electric mixer, beat the egg whites until they form stiff peaks, about 7 minutes. Beat in the granulated sugar until the meringue is thick and glossy white. In a small bowl using a wire whisk, combine the confectioners' sugar and ground almonds. With a curved rubber spatula or long metal spoon, fold the dry mixture into the meringue in a figure-8 pattern until the meringue is smooth and uniform in color.

Fit a pastry bag with a plain 3/8-inch (1-cm) diameter tip. On one of the prepared baking sheets, starting with the inside curl of an apostrophe, pipe outwards left, loop up, then spiral down and stop by poking the tip into the meringue and quickly lifting up; you should have a 3-inch-long apostrophe. Repeat with the remaining meringue, leaving about 1 inch between each apostrophe and refilling the pastry bag as necessary.

Bake until the meringues are dry to the touch and lightly browned, about 25 to 30 minutes, then remove them from the oven and let them cool on the baking sheets.

While the meringues cool, melt the chocolate in the top of a double boiler, or in a heat-safe bowl set over a saucepan of simmering water. Scoop the caramel into a microwave-safe bowl and heat it up in the microwave for 30 seconds on high heat.

Using a spoon, drip some warm caramel into the inner coil of each apostrophe. Holding each apostrophe by its "tail," dip and roll the top edge into the melted chocolate to lightly line the top curve of the apostrophe. Return the chocolate-dipped meringues to the parchment paper to cool and harden. Store them in an airtight container at room temperature for up to 2 days.

Polka Dots

Made by beating hot sugar syrup into egg whites for a high-gloss finish, these tiny meringues look great as cake decorations or as sweet nibbles. Package them for parties as they are, or sandwich them together with Swiss Meringue Buttercream Frosting (page 205), jam, Blood Orange Curd (page 19), Rosemary Caramel (page 24), Mocha Ganache (page 27), chocolate hazelnut spread, or whatever strikes your fancy. These meringues are naturally gluten-free.

MAKES 72 MINIATURE MERINGUES

3   large egg whites
¾   cup (160 g) granulated sugar
1   tablespoon light corn syrup
2   tablespoons water
     Gel food coloring

Preheat the oven to 175°F (80°C). Cut two pieces of parchment to fit two large baking sheets. Outline 36 small (1¼-inch/3-cm) circles on the parchment, ½ inch apart, then flip the paper over and place each piece on a large baking sheet. Have ready four small bowls. If you prefer your meringues to be perfect circles, fit four disposable pastry bags with ½-inch (1.25-cm) round tips or plain couplers, or snip off the corners of four sealable plastic bags on the diagonal; set those aside.

In the bowl of an electric mixer, beat the egg whites until soft peaks form, about 4 minutes.

Stir the sugar, corn syrup, and water together in a heavy saucepan over medium-high heat. Clamp a candy thermometer to the inside of the pan. As the sugar begins to melt, stir it with a whisk or long-handled wooden spoon. When the sugar comes to a boil, stop stirring and remove the spoon from the pan. Let the syrup cook without stirring until the candy thermometer registers 230°F (112°C), about 4 minutes. Remove the pan from the heat.

When the syrup is ready, turn the mixer to low speed and, using an oven mitt, pour the hot syrup in a steady stream into the egg whites. When all the syrup has been incorporated, increase the mixer speed to high. Beat until the egg whites are thick and glossy white, about 5 minutes more.

Divide the meringue among the four bowls and tint each bowl with a different gel color, blending well with a spatula. Working quickly, transfer each tinted meringue to one of the prepared pastry bags or sealable plastic bags. Twist or seal each bag closed. Pipe the meringue into the circles on the prepared baking sheet. If you want meringue without peaks, smooth the surface of each circle with a moistened table knife.

Bake for 2½ hours or until the meringues are dry and light to the touch. Turn the oven off and let the meringues dry out in the cooling oven for 1 hour. Use the meringues right away as decoration for cakes and other desserts, or sandwich two meringues together with a filling and serve them on their own. Store them in an airtight container at room temperature for up to 1 week.

Miniature Chocolate Soufflés

There's something about a chocolate soufflé that entrances even the most experienced cooks. When my culinary book club read and cooked from One Soufflé at a Time: A Memoir of Food and France *by Anne Willan, I was intrigued by Anne's description of how she produced soufflés at dinner parties when she lived in Washington, D.C., in the 1980s. She would get up from the table after the main course, whisk the egg whites in a copper bowl, and 45 minutes later bring the soufflé to the table. For today's shorter timetables, her smaller soufflés work really well. Before my book club friends arrived, I melted the chocolate mixture in a saucepan and set it aside. After we had our main course, I got up from the table, beat the egg whites with my electric mixer, folded in the chocolate, and popped it all in the oven. Voilà! Ten minutes later I served these miniature soufflés, and we all said, "Ahhhh." Adapted from a recipe by Anne Willan.*

MAKES 4 (1-CUP/250-ML) OR 8 (½-CUP/125-ML) SOUFFLÉS

2   tablespoons unsalted butter, melted, for the ramekins

4   ounces (110 g) dark bittersweet chocolate, chopped

½   cup (125 ml) heavy whipping cream

3   large egg yolks

1½   tablespoons rum or cognac

5   large egg whites

3   tablespoons granulated sugar

    Confectioners' sugar, for dusting

Brush the inside of four (8-ounce/250-ml) ramekins or eight (4-ounce/125-ml) ramekins with melted butter and place them on a baking sheet; set aside.

For the chocolate mixture, combine the bittersweet chocolate and cream in a saucepan over low heat, whisking until the chocolate has melted and blended with the cream. Remove the pan from the heat and whisk in the egg yolks and rum until the mixture thickens slightly. Cover and set the chocolate mixture aside at room temperature for at least 30 minutes and up to 2 hours.

Thirty minutes before you want to serve the soufflés, preheat the oven to 425°F (220°C).

In the bowl of an electric mixer, beat the egg whites until stiff peaks form. Add the sugar and beat until the meringue is thick and glossy white, about 7 minutes total.

(recipe continues)

Using a rubber spatula, fold 1 cup (250 ml) of the meringue into the chocolate mixture in the saucepan, until the chocolate has lightened in color. Then fold the chocolate mixture into the egg whites until the mixture is lightly blended and just slightly streaked.

Spoon the soufflé mixture into the prepared ramekins. Run the tip of your finger around the perimeter of the soufflé mixture in each ramekin to make a moat (this helps the soufflé rise and not fall over the edge of the ramekin).

Keeping the ramekins on the baking sheet, transfer them to the oven and bake the large ramekins for 9 minutes and the smaller ones for 7 minutes, or until the soufflés wobble slightly when you gently shake the baking sheet. Remove the soufflés from the oven and dust each one with confectioners' sugar. Serve each soufflé on a napkin-lined dessert plate so they don't slip, and warn your guests that the ramekins are hot.

SO HAPPY TOGETHER

Miniature Chocolate Soufflés
+ Orange Ramekins

It may not seem possible, but there is one more little thing you can do to make these soufflés taste even more fabulous. According to a study by Oxford University and the Polytechnic University of Valencia, hot chocolate actually tastes more chocolaty when you sip it from an orange mug, as opposed to mugs in other colors. Warm, cheerful, optimistic orange paired with rich, comforting chocolate seems to be greater than the sum of its parts. So why not bake these soufflés in orange ramekins?

Raspberry Soufflés

With the raspberry purée already made and chilled ahead of time, you can provide a dramatic ending to dinner with friends by making these raspberry soufflés, which are naturally gluten-free. All you do is whip the egg whites with sugar, blend them with the raspberry purée, and bake. The texture of these soufflés is more marshmallow- and mousse-like than a traditional soufflé made with pastry cream. These raspberry soufflés are also delicious served with fresh raspberries and/or a crisp sugar cookie for "dunking."

1   tablespoon unsalted butter, melted, for the ramekins

1   tablespoon granulated sugar, for the ramekins

RASPBERRY PURÉE

1   (12-ounce/340-g) package frozen raspberries

⅓   cup (67 g) granulated sugar

1   tablespoon cornstarch

1   teaspoon rosewater or freshly squeezed lemon juice

SOUFFLÉS

5   large egg whites

⅓   cup (67 g) granulated sugar

Brush the insides of eight (4-ounce/125-ml) ramekins or sturdy teacups with the melted butter and sprinkle them with the 1 tablespoon of sugar. Place the ramekins on a baking sheet; set aside.

For the Raspberry Purée, heat the frozen raspberries in a medium saucepan over medium-high heat, stirring occasionally, until they are warm and soft, about 4 minutes. Using a wooden spoon, push the raspberries through a fine-mesh sieve into a medium bowl; discard the solids left in the sieve. Rinse out the saucepan. Transfer the raspberry purée to the saucepan and whisk in the sugar and cornstarch. Cook, whisking constantly, until the purée thickens enough so you can see the bottom of the saucepan between whisking strokes. Whisk in the rosewater. Remove the pan from the heat and set it aside to cool at room temperature, or transfer the purée to an airtight container and store it in the refrigerator for up to 3 days.

Preheat the oven to 350°F (180°C). In the bowl of an electric mixer, beat the egg whites until they hold stiff peaks, about 4 minutes. Beat in the sugar until the meringue is thick and glossy white, about 7 minutes total. With a rubber spatula, fold in the Raspberry Purée in a figure-8 pattern until the soufflé mixture turns a solid, medium shade of pink. Spoon the soufflé mixture into the prepared ramekins. Run the tip of your finger around the perimeter of the soufflé mixture to make a moat (this helps the soufflé rise and not fall over the ramekin edges).

Keeping the ramekins on the baking sheet, transfer the soufflés to the oven and bake them for 10 to 11 minutes or until they wobble slightly when you gently shake the baking sheet.

Remove the soufflés from the oven and dust each one with confectioners' sugar. Serve each soufflé on a napkin-lined dessert plate so they don't slip, and warn your guests that the ramekins are hot.

Teacup Lavender-Lemon Soufflés

When I was at La Varenne Ecole de Cuisine in Paris, I learned to make a Grand Marnier soufflé, which could be a dramatic and delicious end to a fancy dinner party. Although we don't do dinner parties with formal china, crystal, and linens as much today, these poufs of sweet lemon and lavender are a welcome finale to any meal. Choose sturdy teacups that are ovenproof. Baked in larger coffee cups, these soufflés will still rise, but only to the rim of the coffee cup and not much beyond. You can find culinary dried lavender (not for potpourri) online at Penzeys Spices. Infuse the Lavender-Lemon Cream (page 23) for at least 1 hour before making the soufflés.

MAKES 8 (4-OUNCE/125-ML) TEACUP SOUFFLÉS

2 tablespoons unsalted butter, melted, for the teacups

2 tablespoons granulated sugar, for the teacups

TEACUP LAVENDER-LEMON SOUFFLÉ

6 large egg whites

⅓ cup (67 g) granulated sugar

1 recipe Lavender-Lemon Cream (page 23), prepared, freshly made or at room temperature

  Confectioners' sugar or colored sprinkles, for dusting

Brush the insides of eight ovenproof teacups with the melted butter and dust them with the 2 tablespoons of granulated sugar; tap out the excess sugar into the sink. Place the teacups on a baking sheet. Set the saucers aside.

Thirty minutes before you want to serve the soufflés, preheat the oven to 425°F (220°C).

In the bowl of an electric mixer, beat the egg whites until they hold stiff peaks, about 4 minutes. Beat in the sugar until the meringue is thick and glossy white, about 7 minutes total. Using a rubber spatula, fold a third of the meringue into the Lavender-Lemon Cream in a figure-8 pattern until the pastry cream has lightened in color. Then fold the pastry cream into the egg whites, moving the spatula in a figure-8 pattern until the mixture is lightly blended and just slightly streaked. Spoon the soufflé mixture into the prepared teacups. Run the tip of your finger around the perimeter of the soufflé mixture to make a moat (this helps the soufflé rise and not fall over the teacup).

(recipe continues)

Keeping the teacups on the baking sheet, transfer the soufflés to the oven and bake them for 10 to 11 minutes or until they wobble slightly when you gently shake the baking sheet.

Remove the soufflés from the oven and dust each one with confectioners' sugar. Serve each soufflé on a napkin-lined dessert plate so they don't slip, and warn your guests that the ramekins are hot.

○ ···················· **VARIATIONS** ···················· ○

MAKE LIMONCELLO, Coffee, or Chocolate Teacup Soufflés simply by using the different Pastry Cream variations on page 23. The soufflé method remains the same.

SO HAPPY TOGETHER

Lavender + Lemon

Aromatic, slightly bitter lavender and sour lemon is an ancient combination that goes back to Roman times. Lavender is deep; lemon is sassy. Both can be overpowering without a little sweetness. They share garden values, love the sun, and taste wonderful in a soufflé.

Blackberry Floating Islands with Orange–Szechuan Pepper Custard

As land-locked Midwesterners, my family has always gone the opposite direction on vacation. We love to be surrounded by water. Perhaps that's the appeal of a dessert that looks like a meringue island surrounded by a sea of homemade pouring custard. The custard, made with orange zest and Szechuan peppercorns (available online or at Penzeys), is inspired by a recipe by David Lebowitz. It is both aromatic and slightly tongue-tingling, and it is a great pairing with fresh berries and sweet, cloud-like meringue. There's a special satisfaction gained by using egg yolks for the custard and the same amount of whites for the meringue, a pleasing symmetry for the baker. Traditionalists might poach the meringue in milk, but to me, it tastes even better baked, which is a much easier method. Infuse the milk for the pouring custard about an hour before making the custard, and keep it chilled until serving.

○ ·········· MAKES 6 SERVINGS ·········· ○

ORANGE–SZECHUAN PEPPER POURING CUSTARD

- 2   cups (500 ml) whole milk
-      Zest of 3 oranges (about 3 tablespoons)
- 1   teaspoon Szechuan peppercorns, crushed (substitute green cardamom pods, whole cloves, or whole coriander seeds)
- 3   large egg yolks
- ¼   cup (50 g) granulated sugar
- 1   to 2 tablespoons Grand Marnier or ¼ teaspoon orange oil (optional)

FOR THE PAN

- 2   tablespoons unsalted butter
- 2   tablespoons granulated sugar

FLOATING ISLANDS

- 3   large egg whites
- ⅓   cup (67 g) granulated sugar
- 1   teaspoon vanilla extract
- 12   ounces (340 g) fresh blackberries, blueberries, black raspberries, or other berry in season

For the Orange–Szechuan Pepper Pouring Custard, heat the milk, orange zest, and Szechuan pepper in a medium saucepan over medium-high heat until bubbles form around the perimeter, about 3 minutes. Remove the pan from the heat, cover it, and let the milk infuse for 1 hour.

In another medium saucepan, whisk together the egg yolks and sugar. Strain the infused milk through a fine-mesh sieve into the egg yolk mixture and whisk well to combine. Place the pan over low heat and bring the mixture to a boil, whisking

(recipe continues)

occasionally. Boil the mixture, whisking constantly, until the custard thickens enough to coat the back of a spoon, about 5 minutes. Remove the pan from the heat. Taste, then stir in the Grand Marnier or orange oil, if you want a more pronounced orange flavor. Set the custard aside. If you are making the custard ahead, transfer it to an airtight container and store it in the refrigerator for up to 2 days before serving.

When you are ready to bake, preheat the oven to 275°F (140°C). Arrange the oven racks in the middle and bottom positions. Coat a 9-inch (23-cm) square baking pan with the butter and sprinkle with the 2 tablespoons of sugar.

For the Floating Islands, in the bowl of an electric mixer, beat the egg whites until soft peaks form, about 4 minutes.

Add the sugar to the bowl and beat until stiff peaks form, about 7 minutes total. Beat in the vanilla.

Carefully pipe or spoon six "islands" of meringue, about 2 inches apart, onto the prepared baking pan. Fill a roasting pan or a large, shallow baking pan with hot water to a depth of 1 inch (2.5 cm). Sit the prepared baking pan on the middle rack of the oven and position the pan of water on the lower rack.

Bake the meringues for 25 to 30 minutes, or until they are firm and lightly browned. Remove the pan from the oven. To serve, divide the custard among six shallow serving bowls, and top each serving with a warm meringue island and ½ cup (125 ml) of blackberries.

Chapter Four

COOKIES

EVER SINCE AUTHOR AMELIA SIMMONS used the term "cookie" in the first published American cookbook in 1796, we've had a thing for these little treats. Over 93 percent of us have a cookie at least once a month, confirms Land O' Lakes, a butter brand based in Minnesota that takes the pulse of cookie lovers from time to time. According to their research, 70 percent of Americans prefer chocolate as the primary flavoring, while about 50 percent also like a buttery flavor. Seventy percent of cookie bakers make cookies for someone they care about, so that the bakers as well as the recipients have positive feelings. We bake around 10 billion cookies for the holidays—that's 10 billion little ways to be happy, but who's counting?

We don't know why, but cookies seem to make everything better. Creativity Kickstarters (page 90) served with aromatic Sweet Orange Mint Gremolata can prompt ideas in a meeting. Chocolate Chunk Cookies (page 102), Chocolate Peanut Butter Cookies (page 110), or Homemade Oreos (page 104)—do you sense a chocolate theme here?—can restore you after a hard day at school or work. Classic Sugar Cookies (page 95) or Confetti Cookies (page 94) communicate "I love you" or "Let's celebrate" any day, anywhere.

Cookies are also great connectors. When Dan Barnett, a project engineer in Chicago, had to attend meetings that included front office people and those who worked the factory floor, he stumbled upon the best ice-breaker ever—homemade cookies. He started making different cookies and bringing them into work every week for a year and a half. "It was a way of greasing the social wheels," he says. "Cookies helped connect the dots between management, the custom fabricators, and the sales people," he says. Chitchat Bars (page 109) are a good cookie to get people talking, as they taste great, yet are gluten-free and vegan as well. Who could resist?

"When my now-husband and I met in high school, I would bake him cookies all the time," says Maria Siriano who bakes and blogs at Sift & Whisk in Columbus, Ohio. "I joke that that's why he has stayed with me all these years! When my husband tells me that something I've baked is his new favorite thing, it totally makes my day."

Sometimes, we're happiest when we make the absolute best version of a traditional cookie. Try Apricot and Pistachio Rugelach (page 93), Gingerbread Cut-Outs with a little fresh ginger (page 98), or Browned Butter Cookies with Rosemary Caramel Drizzle (page 100) on a platter garnished with sugared rosemary branches. Give a cookie quilt (page 97) to friends and neighbors or use edible transfer papers to give your sugar cookies a custom look.

Cookies are easy to make, easy to bake, easy to give, and so delicious to eat warm from the oven. So indulge a little bit. It's good for you.

"C is for cookie. That's good enough for me."

Cookie Monster

Creativity Kickstarters

"There has to be a better way!" I said to myself. I was at a brainstorming meeting. To help us along, the group brought out a plastic tray full of pallid sugar cookies that tasted as uninteresting as they looked. One tiny bite and I was all out of ideas. I went home and took out my bottle of Aura Cacia "Creative Juice," a blend of non-culinary essential oils that includes bergamot and cardamom. I sniffed its wonderful aroma. The light bulb went on, and the result is these soft sugar cookies, flavored with cardamom. The final touch is an aromatizing gremolata with citrus zest, orange mint, and raw sugar that practically shouts "fresh and new." If the ideas don't flow after that, it's not my fault.

MAKES ABOUT 36 COOKIES

SOFT SUGAR COOKIE DOUGH

2¾	cups (335 g) unbleached all-purpose flour
½	teaspoon baking soda
¼	teaspoon fine salt
½	cup (125 ml) sour cream, at room temperature
½	cup (113 g) unsalted butter, at room temperature
1	cup (200 g) granulated sugar
1	large egg
½	teaspoon vanilla extract
1	tablespoon ground cardamom

ORANGE GLAZE

1	cup (120 g) confectioners' sugar
1	teaspoon freshly grated orange zest
3	tablespoons freshly squeezed orange juice

SWEET ORANGE MINT GREMOLATA

1	tablespoon finely chopped fresh orange mint, spearmint, or mint leaves
½	teaspoon freshly grated orange zest
½	teaspoon freshly grated lemon zest
¼	cup (50 g) raw sugar

Preheat the oven to 350°F (180°C). Line two large baking sheets with parchment paper and set them aside.

For the cookies, whisk together the flour, baking soda, and salt in a medium bowl. In the bowl of an electric mixer, cream together the sour cream, butter, and sugar until light and fluffy, about 5 minutes. Beat in the egg, vanilla, and cardamom. With the mixer running on low speed, mix in the dry ingredients, one-third at a time, until you have a smooth, soft dough. Pinch off a 1-tablespoon-sized ball of dough, roll it gently in your hands, flatten it into a 1-inch-thick disc, and place it on one of the prepared baking sheets. Repeat with the remaining dough, spacing the discs 1½ inches (4 cm) apart on the baking sheets.

Bake the cookies for 7 to 9 minutes or until they are just firm to the touch and slightly golden at the edges. Remove the cookies from the oven and let them cool on the baking sheets.

For the Orange Glaze, in a medium bowl, whisk together the confectioners' sugar, orange zest, and orange juice until smooth. Turn each cookie upside down and dip the top in the glaze. Turn the glazed cookies upright and place them on the baking sheet again to dry.

For the Gremolata, in a medium bowl, muddle the orange mint , citrus zests, and sugar with a muddler or with the handle of wooden spoon until the sugar is suffused with color and aroma. Sprinkle the gremolata over the glazed cookies and let them rest until the glaze has set, about 30 minutes. Store the cookies at room temperature in an airtight container for up to 3 days.

Apricot and Pistachio Rugelach

Rugelach, the rolled crescents of pastry enclosing a sweet filling, can be another blank canvas for your cookie creativity. Switch the apricot preserves for cherry or plum, the dried apricots for dried sour cherries or snipped dried plums, and the pistachios for almonds, and you've got two more versions of a tender flavorful cookie that keeps well.

MAKES 60 COOKIES

ALMOND RUGELACH DOUGH

7	ounces (199 g) almond paste
2	cups (250 g) unbleached all-purpose flour
¼	teaspoon fine salt
1	(8-ounce/226-g) package cream cheese, cut into ½-inch (1.25-cm) pieces, at room temperature
1	cup (227 g) cold unsalted butter, cut into ½-inch (1.25-cm) pieces

APRICOT AND PISTACHIO FILLING

1	cup (150 g) dried apricots, snipped into small pieces with kitchen scissors
1	cup (113 g) coarsely chopped roasted, unsalted shelled pistachios
1	(12-ounce/340-g) jar apricot preserves
1	large egg, beaten
	Raw or turbinado sugar, for sprinkling

For the Almond Rugelach Dough, place the almond paste in a food processor or a bowl with a pastry blender and process or cut it until you have a uniform mixture with no large lumps. Add the flour and salt and process or cut in the mixture to combine. Add the cream cheese and butter and process or cut the mixture until it resembles coarse crumbs. Transfer the dough to a lightly floured surface and knead for 1 minute until it comes together into a smooth ball. Divide the dough into fourths, wrap each portion in plastic wrap, and refrigerate for 30 minutes.

For the Apricot and Pistachio Filling, in a small bowl, combine the apricots and the pistachios; set aside.

When you are ready to bake, preheat the oven to 375°F (190°C). Line two large baking sheets with parchment paper and set them aside.

Remove the dough from the refrigerator and roll each portion into a 9-inch (23-cm) circle. Evenly trim the edges, using a 9-inch (23-cm) pie plate or round cake pan as a template, and reserve the trimmings to gather together for a fifth circle of dough. Spread each dough circle with 3 tablespoons of the apricot preserves, leaving a 1-inch (2.5-cm) border. Sprinkle ⅓ cup (75 ml) of the Apricot and Pistachio Filling onto each circle. Using a pizza wheel or a sharp knife, cut each dough circle into 12 equal pie-shaped wedges. Starting at the wide side, roll up each wedge into a crescent. Place the crescents on the prepared baking sheets, about 1 inch apart. Brush each crescent with beaten egg and sprinkle with sugar.

Bake the cookies for 21 to 23 minutes or until they are puffed and golden. Remove the baking sheets from the oven and transfer the rugelach to wire racks to cool. These cookies keep well at room temperature in an airtight container for up to 2 weeks.

Confetti Cookies

My sister Julie, who lives in Atlanta, loves to give small containers of tiny chocolate chip cookies known as Nam's Bits as a casual thank-you gift. But I'm a sucker for a good butter cookie like this one that has been in our family for a long, long time. The versatile dough can be tinted, then pressed into any shape the occasion demands— flowers, Christmas trees, hearts, or swirls. I love the dough formed into small cylinders, then rolled in a bed of colored sprinkles, and finally cut into tiny rounds to bake. Package these little cookies in small bags tied with a bow or put them in small tins for a charming favor or gift. Roll them in custom-colored sprinkles for a wedding, baby shower, or birthday party. You can freeze the dough for up to 3 months, then just slice and bake it when the occasion demands. You can also store baked cookies in airtight containers at room temperature for up to 2 weeks or in the freezer for up to 3 months.

MAKES ABOUT 36 COOKIES

1   cup (227 g) unsalted butter, at room temperature
½   cup (100 g) granulated sugar
1   teaspoon almond extract or vanilla extract
       Gel food coloring (optional)
2⅓   cups (292 g) unbleached all-purpose flour
½   teaspoon fine salt
½   cup (125 ml) Homemade Colored Sprinkles (page 35) or storebought

Preheat the oven to 300°F (150°C). Line two large baking sheets with parchment paper and set them aside.

In the bowl of an electric mixer, cream together the butter, sugar, almond extract, and food coloring until light and fluffy, about 5 minutes. Sift the flour and salt into a medium bowl. Beat the flour mixture into the butter mixture, ½ cup (63 g) at a time, until you have a smooth, thick dough.

Divide the dough in half. Wrap one of the dough halves in plastic wrap and keep it in the refrigerator while you make the first batch of cookies.

Have ready one large (11 x 17-inch/28 x 43-cm) sheet of parchment paper on your work surface. Divide the dough into four portions. With the palms of your hands, roll each portion to form a long cylinder about 1 inch (2.5 cm) in diameter. Sprinkle a line of colored sprinkles along the length of the cylinder and roll the cookie dough in the sprinkles, making sure to coat the dough evenly. With a sharp knife, cut the cylinder of dough into 1-inch/2.5-cm-thick pieces and place them on a prepared baking sheet about 1 inch (2.5 cm) apart. Repeat with the remaining dough and sprinkles.

Bake for 10 to 12 minutes, or until the cookies are slightly golden but not brown. Remove the cookies from the oven and let them cool completely on the baking sheet. Store them in an airtight container at room temperature for up to 1 week.

Classic Sugar Cookies

A standout sugar cookie starts with a dough that tastes good and performs well under adverse conditions (like a pack of preschoolers in a small kitchen). This one definitely does. The dough has a buttery, vanilla-scented flavor; is easy to roll out; and doesn't spread during baking. The dough can also be frozen for up to 3 months before baking. Once the dough is made, the process of cutting out the sugar cookies is a great opportunity for nostalgia and collecting. In our family, making holiday sugar cookies with the kids has always been fun—and messy. And I love my collection of cookie cutters, from ones made by my late father-in-law to those made by Bill and Betsy Cukla of Hammer Song, who, as their motto states, fashion "Cookie Cutters to Make You Laugh, Cry, Giggle or Remember." For the best results, sift the flour first, then measure it. Rolling out the dough between two sheets of parchment paper keeps the mess to a minimum and results in more tender cookies without that extra flour. After painting the cookies with Cookie Paint, you can also apply edible transfer wafer papers in just about any pattern, using a little bit of corn syrup to "glue" them on the cookie (see page 96). You can find these transfers at fancyflours.com or on Etsy. You can find meringue powder at hobby, craft, and cake supply stores or online.

MAKES 30 (3-INCH/7.5-CM) COOKIES

CLASSIC SUGAR COOKIE DOUGH

3   cups (285 g) sifted unbleached all-purpose flour

1½   teaspoons baking powder

1   teaspoon fine salt

1   cup (227 g) unsalted butter, at room temperature

1   cup (200 g) granulated sugar

1   large egg

1   teaspoon vanilla extract, almond extract, or lemon extract

COOKIE PAINT

2   tablespoons meringue powder

¼   cup (60 ml) cold water

1   teaspoon vanilla extract, almond extract, lemon extract, or raspberry extract

2   cups (240 g) confectioners' sugar

    Gel food coloring

For the Classic Sugar Cookie Dough, sift the flour (again) with the baking powder and salt into a medium bowl; set the bowl aside. In the bowl of an electric mixer, cream together the butter and sugar until the mixture becomes very pale and fluffy, about 3 minutes. Beat in the egg and extract. Beat in the dry ingredients, one-third at a time, until the dough just comes together. Gather the dough into a ball, turn it out onto a lightly floured surface, and knead it for 1 minute. Cut the dough in half and form each half into a flattened disc. Use the dough right away or wrap the discs and freeze them for up to 3 months. Let the dough come to room temperature before rolling it out.

When you are ready to bake the cookies, preheat the oven to 350°F (180°C). Line two large baking sheets with parchment paper and set them aside.

(recipe continues)

Have ready two large (11 x 17-inch/28 x 43-cm) sheets of parchment paper or two silicon baking mats. Place one of the sheets of parchment or silicone baking mats on a flat surface. Place one disc of dough in the center and cover it with the second piece of parchment or silicon baking mat. Roll out the dough to a ¼-inch (6-mm) thickness. Cut out the cookie shapes and place them close to each other on one of the prepared baking sheets. Repeat this process with the same parchment paper or silicone mats and the second disc of dough.

Bake the cookies until the edges are golden brown, about 8 to 10 minutes. Remove the cookies from the oven and let them cool on the baking sheets for a few minutes, then transfer them to wire racks to cool completely.

For the Cookie Paint, in a medium bowl, whisk together the meringue powder, water, extract, and confectioners' sugar until the mixture is smooth and has a paint-like consistency. Use a gel color of your choice to tint the paint in the bowl, or, if you like, divide the paint among separate bowls and tint each bowl a different color. Using a clean, large watercolor, paint, or pastry brush, paint the cookies and let them dry for at least 1 hour before serving. Serve right away or store the cookies at room temperature in an airtight container for up to 1 week.

USING EDIBLE TRANSFER WAFER PAPERS

Edible transfer wafer papers can be used to transform your sugar cookies into vintage flower seed packets or to adorn them with your favorite china pattern, botanical prints, or any other pattern you like. All it takes is a scanner, a designated printer with edible inks, and edible transfer wafer paper. Creating edible transfer wafer papers has become a cottage industry with crafters on sites like Etsy. Edible transfer wafer papers dissolve in moisture, which is why you can eat them.

To use these papers, cut the sugar cookies to fit the transfer. Bake and ice your cookies with Cookie Paint, royal icing, or fondant and make sure they're completely dry. Brush a little light corn syrup on the back of each transfer and "glue" it to the cookie, pressing the transfer with dry fingers. Turn each cookie over, wafer paper–side down, on a piece of parchment paper and let them dry for 30 minutes. Then turn the cookies right-side up and let them dry for another 12 hours. After that, you can add other decorations such as buttercream frosting borders or sugar pearls attached with clear piping gel. Do not refrigerate.

Cookie + Quilt

I was experimenting with this dough at the same time I interviewed Scott Heffley, the senior curator of paintings who is restoring El Greco's *The Penitent Magdalen* for the Nelson-Atkins Museum of Art in Kansas City. On weekends, Heffley loves the thrill of the hunt at flea markets, estate sales, and antique shops. "I like things that have a little spirit," he says, "that sort of capture the energy of the maker or the time period." That impulse led him to collect African-American quilts, which look like jazz on cloth. In Heffley's book *Bold Improvisation: Searching for African-American Quilts*, one quilt that he calls "Ocean Wave Variation" stood out for me. It's a rectangular quilt made up of squares that are bisected on the diagonal. It was simple enough to try with a rectangle of Classic Sugar Cookie Dough. I simply rolled out a rectangle and trimmed the edges, then used a pizza wheel to cut the rectangle into squares. I lifted the parchment paper to move the cookie quilt onto a baking sheet, and baked it without separating the cookies. After they cooled, I used cookie paint in four different colors to make my own bisected squares and add a bit of pattern here and there. It was easy to do, delicious to eat, pleasing to me, and a hit at the meeting the next day.

Gingerbread Cut-Outs

I am still charmed by an old House Beautiful *magazine story that shows gingerbread cookie animals, stars, and angels displayed on tiered glass cake stands with the description: "Herds of curlicue-frosted animal cookies star briefly in our Christmas dessert buffet, then bite the dust." More recently, I saved a photo of a Victorian-style gingerbread cookie house decked out for the holidays from Bobbette & Belle Artisanal Pastries in Toronto. Whimsical, fun, timeless, and delicious, these cookies have a deep, dark, fresh-and-dried gingery flavor and perform well as cut-out parts of a gingerbread house or as individual cookies. My favorite cut-outs include a wooly sheep, a sprightly squirrel accompanied by tiny acorns, and a slightly off-kilter house. Use Sugar Icing for white details and apply Browned Butter Frosting so that the edges of the cookies show. Rolling out the dough between sheets of parchment paper cuts down on the mess. You can make and bake the undecorated cookies up to 3 months before you need them and keep them in the freezer. Make sure you thaw the cookies completely before decorating.*

MAKES ABOUT 48 COOKIES

GINGERBREAD COOKIE DOUGH

½   cup (113 g) unsalted butter, at room temperature
½   cup (100 g) granulated sugar
¼   teaspoon fine salt
½   cup (125 ml) molasses, pure cane syrup, or dark sorghum
1   large egg
1   tablespoon cider vinegar
1   tablespoon grated fresh ginger
3   cups (500 g) unbleached all-purpose flour
¾   teaspoon baking soda
1   teaspoon ground cinnamon
2   teaspoons ground ginger

BROWNED BUTTER FROSTING

¾   cup (170 g) unsalted butter, cut into pieces
3   cups (360 g) confectioners' sugar, sifted
¼   teaspoon fine salt
2   teaspoons vanilla extract
⅓   cup (75 ml) heavy whipping cream

SUGAR ICING

4   tablespoons (60 g) unsalted butter, at room temperature
1   pound (454 g) confectioners' sugar
1   tablespoon vanilla extract
2   tablespoons whole milk, plus more as needed

For the Gingerbread Cookie Dough, in the bowl of an electric mixer, cream together the butter, sugar, and salt until the mixture is fluffy and pale in color, about 4 minutes. Beat in the molasses, egg, cider vinegar, and fresh ginger until smooth. Sift the flour, baking soda, cinnamon, and ground ginger together into a large bowl. Beat the dry ingredients into the molasses mixture, one-third at a time, until you have a stiff dough. Divide the dough in half and press each half into a disc. Use the dough right away, or wrap it in plastic wrap and store it in the refrigerator for up to 3 days or in the freezer for up to 3 months.

When you are ready to bake, preheat the oven to 375°F (190°C). Line two large baking sheets with parchment paper and set them aside.

Have ready two large (11 x 17-inch/28 x 43-cm) sheets of parchment paper or two silicon baking mats. Place one of the sheets of parchment or silicone baking mats on a flat surface. Place one disc of dough in the center and cover it with the second piece of parchment or silicon baking mat. Roll out the dough to a ¼-inch (6-mm) thickness. Cut out your cookie shapes and place them on a prepared baking sheet about ½ inch (1.25 cm) apart. Repeat this process with the same parchment papers or silicone mats and the second disc of dough.

Bake for 8 to 10 minutes or until they are firm to the touch and lightly browned at the edges. Remove the cookies from the oven and let them cool on the baking sheets for a few minutes, then transfer them to wire racks to cool completely. (You can freeze the baked cookies for up to 3 months before decorating.)

For the Browned Butter Frosting, melt the butter in a medium saucepan over medium-high heat until it begins to turn a golden brown color, about 5 to 7 minutes, then immediately remove the pan from the heat. Watch the pan carefully, as the butter can easily burn. Whisk the confectioners' sugar, salt, and vanilla into the browned butter until smooth, then whisk in the cream, a little at a time, until the frosting reaches a spreadable consistency.

For the Sugar Icing, in the bowl of an electric mixer, beat together the butter, confectioners' sugar, vanilla, and milk until smooth. The icing should hold its shape but be soft enough to pipe through a pastry bag. (If you like, save a very small amount and color it robin's egg blue to make eyes for snowmen or animal shapes.) Fit a pastry bag with a small #1 or #2 tip and fill the pastry bag with the white Sugar Icing.

To decorate the cookies, spread the Browned Butter Frosting on some cookies to that you can still see the dark brown outline of the cookie. Pipe dots, curlicues, stripes, and other details with the Sugar Icing. Using a toothpick, make a small dot of robin's egg blue icing, if you like, for eyes. Let the icing and frosting harden for about 1 hour before storing the cookies between layers of parchment paper in cookie tins for up to 2 weeks.

Browned Butter Cookies with Rosemary Caramel Drizzle

These rich cookies underline one of the main concepts of Bake Happy. If a baked treat is full of flavor, you can feel satisfied nibbling one or two, so you're less likely to polish off a platter full. The vanilla bean adds a luxurious flavor to the butter, which is accentuated by a finishing drizzle of Rosemary Caramel (page 24). If you like, you can make the caramel ahead; it will keep in an airtight container in the refrigerator for up to 2 weeks.

MAKES ABOUT 48 COOKIES

1	cup (227 g) unsalted butter, at room temperature
1	vanilla bean
½	cup (100 g) granulated sugar
2¼	cups (281 g) unbleached all-purpose flour
1	teaspoon fine salt
1	cup Rosemary Caramel (page 24)

Melt the butter in a heavy saucepan over medium-high heat. Clip a candy thermometer to the inside of the pan. Slit the vanilla bean in half lengthwise and scrape the seeds into the melted butter. Continue cooking until the butter bubbles, then turns medium brown with dark flecks, at around 250°F (120°C) on the candy thermometer, about 8 to 10 minutes. Remove the pan from the heat and let it cool until the butter is opaque, about 15 minutes.

Line two large baking sheets with parchment paper and set them aside. Preheat the oven to 325°F (160°C).

In the bowl of an electric mixer, cream the browned butter and sugar until fluffy, about 4 minutes. Add the flour and salt and beat until you have a stiff dough that comes together into a ball. Divide the dough in half.

Have ready one large (11 x 17-inch/28 x 43-cm) sheet of parchment paper or one silicone baking mat. Place on a flat surface. With the palms of your hands, roll each dough half into a 16-inch-/40-cm-long log. Cut each log into ¼-inch (6-mm) slices and arrange the slices on the prepared baking sheets, about ½ inch (1.25 cm) apart.

Bake for 25 to 28 minutes or until the cookies are just slightly firm to the touch. Remove the cookies from the oven and let them cool on the baking sheets.

Scoop the caramel into a microwave-safe container and microwave it for 30 seconds on high heat, then pour it into a plastic squeeze bottle. Drizzle each cookie generously with the warm caramel. The caramel will stay soft, so don't stack cookies on top of each other. Serve immediately. Store the cookies in an airtight container at room temperature for up to 1 week.

SO HAPPY TOGETHER

Rosemary + Sugar

Sugared fresh rosemary adds a festive garnish to a platter of these rich cookies. Simply brush or dip the branches in beaten egg white or reconstituted powdered egg white, sprinkle with sparkling sugar, and let them dry.

Chocolate Chunk Cookies

Erin Brown of Dolce Bakery in Prairie Village, Kansas, welcomes the relaxed pace of baking in her home kitchen. Brown's husband, a professional athlete, "trains like a beast," she says, but he saves room for her Chocolate Chunk Cookies, adapted here, dipped in an affogato. For these cookies, bigger is better to achieve a gooey interior and a crispy exterior. If you want to work ahead, mix the dough and place the unbaked cookies on a baking sheet. Stick the whole thing in the freezer for 30 minutes, then remove the unbaked cookies from the baking sheet and freeze them in a sealable plastic bag for up to 3 months. Bake the frozen cookies for about 8 to 12 minutes longer.

MAKES 24 COOKIES

2 cups plus 2 tablespoons (265 g) unbleached all-purpose flour

1 teaspoon baking soda

½ teaspoon fine salt

1½ cups (270 g) semisweet chocolate chunks

1 cup (180 g) large bittersweet chocolate chips

1½ cups (180 g) finely chopped walnuts

1 cup (227 g) unsalted butter, at room temperature

1 cup (220 g) packed dark brown sugar

½ cup (100 g) granulated sugar

2 large eggs

2 teaspoons vanilla extract (or 1 teaspoon vanilla bean paste)

Preheat the oven to 375°F (190°C). Line two large baking sheets with parchment paper and set them aside.

Sift the flour, baking soda, and salt together into a medium bowl; set it aside. In a second medium bowl, combine the chocolate chunks, chocolate chips, and walnuts.

In the bowl of an electric mixer, cream together the butter and sugars until the mixture is light and fluffy, about 4 to 5 minutes. Scrape down the sides of the bowl. Add the eggs, one at a time, beating and scraping after each addition. Beat in the vanilla. Beat in the dry ingredients on low speed, one-quarter at a time, adding the chocolate chip and nut mixture with the last of the flour.

Scoop 2 tablespoons of dough onto the prepared baking sheets for each cookie, spacing them 2 inches (5 cm) apart.

Bake, one pan at a time, until the cookies are browned and crispy at the edges and soft in the middle, about 8 to 10 minutes. Remove the cookies from the oven and let them cool on the baking sheets for a few minutes, then transfer them to wire racks to cool completely. Store the cookies in an airtight container for up to 1 week at room temperature or for up to 3 months in the freezer. To warm the cookies before serving, microwave a frozen cookie on high for 15 to 20 seconds or until it is warm and gooey.

Chocolate Chunk Cookies + Affogato

A warm Chocolate Chunk Cookie dunked in an affogato can elevate a wonderful experience into the unforgettable—if you love coffee. To make an affogato, Italian for "drowned," simply put a scoop of ice cream or gelato in a coffee cup and pour a shot or two of hot espresso over it. Let the ice cream melt just a little, then dunk in a still-warm Chocolate Chunk Cookie.

Homemade Oreos

Let's face it. Oreos can be addictive, as a study by researchers at Connecticut College determined. Nibbling the salty chocolate cookie with its sweet vanilla filling prompts neuronal activation in the "pleasure center" of the brain (or at least it does in lab rats). But we're not lab rats. We're people. So, let's have a homemade, you-know-exactly-what's-in-it treat. Adapted from a recipe by Joanne Chang of Flour Bakery in Boston, this recipe for homemade Oreos can be customized to your taste. Make them bigger or smaller. Color and flavor the filling as you wish. And dunk all you want.

○ ·········· MAKES ABOUT 16 (3-INCH/7.5-CM) SANDWICH COOKIES ·········· ○

COOKIES

1	cup (226 g) unsalted butter, cut into pieces
¾	cup (160 g) granulated sugar
1	cup (175 g) semisweet chocolate chips
1	large egg
1	teaspoon vanilla extract
1½	cups (188 g) unbleached all-purpose flour
¾	cup (88 g) unsweetened cocoa powder
1	teaspoon fine salt
½	teaspoon baking soda

VANILLA FILLING

½	cup (113 g) unsalted butter, at room temperature
1⅔	cups (195 g) confectioners' sugar
⅛	teaspoon fine salt
1	tablespoon whole milk
1	teaspoon vanilla extract
	Gel food coloring (optional)

For the cookies, in a medium saucepan over medium-low heat, whisk together the butter, granulated sugar, and chocolate chips until the butter and chocolate have just melted, about 5 minutes. Remove the pan from the heat and whisk in the egg and vanilla until well blended. Whisk in the flour, cocoa powder, salt, and baking soda until well blended. Let the mixture cool for 15 minutes, then cover the pan and refrigerate the dough for 30 minutes or until it is thick like modeling clay.

Place a 15-inch/38-cm-long sheet of parchment paper on a work surface. Spoon the dough onto the parchment and form it into a 12-inch/30-cm-long log. Roll the parchment paper around the log of dough and work the dough into a smooth cylinder about 10 inches (25 cm) long and 2½ inches (6 cm) in diameter. Wrap the dough in plastic wrap and chill it in the refrigerator for 2 hours or overnight. (You can also wrap and freeze the dough for up to 3 months at this point.)

When you are ready to bake the cookies, preheat the oven to 325°F (160°C). Line two large baking sheets with parchment paper and set them aside.

Remove the cookie dough from the refrigerator and unwrap it. Using a chef's knife, cut the dough into ¼-inch/6-mm-thick slices and arrange the slices 1 inch (2.5 cm) apart on the prepared baking sheets. Bake the cookies on the upper and lower racks in the oven for 11 minutes, then switch the baking sheets and continue baking for another 11 minutes or until the cookies are just firm when pressed gently in the middle. Remove the cookies from the oven and let them cool on the baking sheets for 1 hour. The cookies will firm up as they cool.

For the filling, in the bowl of an electric mixer, beat together the butter, confectioners' sugar, milk, and vanilla until smooth. Add food coloring of your choice, if you wish.

Place about 1 tablespoon of the filling in the center of one cookie, top with another cookie, and gently press in the middle of the top cookie to spread the filling out to the edges. Repeat this process with the remaining filling and cookies.

Serve the cookies immediately or store them in an airtight container at room temperature for up to 3 days.

VARIATIONS

FOR SMALLER COOKIES, form the dough into a 14-inch/36-cm-long cylinder with a 1½-inch (4-cm) diameter. Cut the dough cylinder into ¼-inch (6-mm) slices and bake the cookies for 20 minutes total, switching the baking sheets halfway through baking. Fill the smaller cookies with 2 teaspoons of filling.

FOR COFFEE FILLING, add 1 tablespoon of freshly brewed dark roast coffee in place of the milk.

FOR VANILLA-LAVENDER FILLING, add ¼ teaspoon of dried culinary lavender buds to the filling.

SO HAPPY TOGETHER

Homemade Oreos + Flavored Milk

As a kid, I loved to dunk Oreos in a little cup of coffee flavored with milk and sugar, which my sister and I were allowed to have after dinner. For extra pleasure, dunk your Homemade Oreos in a flavored beverage to match your filling.

Dunk vanilla-filled sandwich cookies in Mint Milk, made by stirring 2 teaspoons of Fresh Herb Syrup (page 30) made with fresh mint into a glass of cold milk. You can also try dunking these in eggnog.

Dunk coffee-filled sandwich cookies in a cup of café au lait or hot chocolate.

Dunk vanilla-lavender-filled sandwich cookies in chamomile or lavender tea.

Black and Whites in Color

Black and white cookies, also known as Half-Moon Cookies, have been a staple of New York City delis for generations. These soft, cake-like cookies have a chocolate-iced side as well as a vanilla-iced side. To those who didn't grow up eating them—like me—they can look and taste sort of ho-hum. But William Greenberg Desserts, a bakery on Madison Avenue, recently changed all that. They now offer custom Black and Whites in fourteen different colors that you can mix and match. Now you're talkin'. I went into my own kitchen, played around with a few recipes, and came up with a lemony cookie that you can dip first in one color icing, then in another. The three custom colors I created that day were turquoise, pink, and soft coral. I took these colorful cookies to my culinary book club gathering that night—a tough crowd of tasters—and my friends gobbled them up.

.... **MAKES 36 COOKIES** ....

COOKIES

1	cup (125 g) unbleached all-purpose flour
1	cup (82 g) cake flour
½	teaspoon baking powder
½	teaspoon fine salt
1	teaspoon freshly grated lemon zest
2	large eggs
¾	cup (160 g) granulated sugar
½	cup (125 ml) whole milk
6	tablespoons (90 g) unsalted butter, melted and cooled
1	teaspoon vanilla extract

ICING

1½	cups (120 g) confectioners' sugar
4½	tablespoons (57 ml) fresh lemon juice (from 1 large lemon)
	Gel food coloring

Preheat the oven to 350°F (180°C). Line two large baking sheets with parchment paper and set them aside.

For the cookies, combine the flours, baking powder, and salt in a small bowl. In the bowl of an electric mixer, beat together the lemon zest, eggs, and sugar until well blended. Add the milk, melted butter, and vanilla and beat until well blended. Add the flour mixture to the egg mixture, one-third at a time, and beat on low speed until a soft dough forms.

Using a 1-tablespoon cookie scoop, drop 24 balls of dough 1 inch (2.5 cm) apart on the prepared baking sheets. Reserve the remaining dough at room temperature for a second batch.

Bake for 7 minutes or until the cookies are lightly browned at the edges and set on top. Remove the cookies from the oven and transfer them to a wire rack to cool. Repeat the process with the remaining dough. Let the cookies cool for 1 hour before icing.

For the icing, whisk the confectioners' sugar and lemon juice together in a medium bowl until smooth. Divide the icing among four bowls and tint each batch a different color. Dip half of each cookie into a colored icing, then let the cookies dry for 30 minutes on wire racks. Dip the other half of each cookie into another color of icing, return the cookies to the wire racks, and let them dry for 1 hour before serving. The cookies will keep in an airtight container at room temperature for up to 3 days.

THE SECRET LANGUAGE OF COLOR

A few years ago, I first came across the idea of color language at the Mii Amo spa in Sedona, Arizona. There, my eye was immediately drawn to a display of small glass bottles filled with two different colored liquids each—turquoise and magenta, gold and violet, olive and coral—from Aura-Soma, a color therapy company based in Sedona. On their web site, www.aurasoma-sedona.com, you can do a free online "reading" to see what your chosen color pairs suggest about your inner life. The colors I chose spoke to me of self-sufficiency, ancient knowledge expressed through the heart, and give and take in love. How about you?

In *Bake Happy*, color is another way to express yourself and make your creation even more appealing. Why not tint your signature frosting coral, if that color pleases you? Why not serve a tart filled with Passion Fruit and Orange Curd (page 20) on a turquoise plate, to enhance your visual pleasure? A pop of unexpected color keeps things fresh and interesting.

Chitchat Bars

My friend Liz Benson, who loves to chat, gave her more laconic husband Tom a pack of "chitchat" cards for Christmas. Each card has a question guaranteed to be a conversation starter. These bars prompt the same flow of communication. When you bring them in to work or to a meeting, they break down social barriers, as unexpected treats generally do. Plus, you can reach almost everyone. On a diet? No problem. Fresh-ginger flavored with a hint of lime, just one good-carb cookie will satisfy. Gluten-free? Yes. Vegan? Check. Delicious? You betcha. Use a microplane grater to make short work of the fresh ginger—you don't even have to peel it.

MAKES 24 BARS

BARS

1	cup (95 g) gluten-free unbleached all-purpose flour blend
1	cup (112 g) almond flour or finely ground almonds
½	teaspoon baking soda
2	teaspoons baking powder
1	teaspoon fine salt
1	teaspoon ground cinnamon
1½	tablespoons ground ginger
1	tablespoon grated fresh ginger
¼	cup (60 ml) water
⅓	cup (104 g) sorghum or molasses
⅓	cup (75 ml) canola oil
1	teaspoon vanilla extract

FRESH LIME ICING

1	cup (120 g) confectioners' sugar, sifted
2	tablespoons vanilla-flavored almond, rice, or soy milk
1	teaspoon freshly grated lime zest

Line a 13 x 9-inch (33 x 23-cm) baking pan with parchment paper so that the paper comes up the sides of the pan. Preheat the oven to 375°F (190°C).

For the bars, in a large bowl, whisk together the flours, baking soda, baking powder, salt, cinnamon, and ground ginger. In a small bowl, whisk together the fresh ginger, water, sorghum, oil, and vanilla until well blended. Pour the sorghum mixture into the dry ingredients and stir with a wooden spoon until you have a soft yet sturdy dough. Spoon and press the dough into the prepared pan.

Bake for 10 to 12 minutes or until the cookie is firm to the touch in the middle of the pan. Remove the cookie from the oven and let it cool for 20 minutes, then cut it into bars using a small, sharp knife. Arrange the cooled bars on a piece of parchment paper on a flat work surface.

For the Fresh Lime Icing, whisk together the confectioners' sugar, almond milk, and lime zest in a medium bowl until smooth. Using the tines of a fork or a whisk, drizzle a pattern of icing over each bar. Let the icing set for 1 hour before serving. Store the bars in an airtight container at room temperature for up to 3 days.

Chocolate Peanut Butter Cookies

Ask and you shall receive. That's what happened to me when I had lunch in the café at Nordstrom and took one bite of a chunky peanut butter cookie dipped halfway in chocolate ganache. Heaven. I asked, and they gave me the cookie recipe, which I have adapted here. The hint of warm cinnamon and chipotle in the chocolate ganache really brings out the roasty-toasty peanut flavor in the cookie. The jury was still out amongst my tasters as to whether they liked the addition of roasted, salted peanuts or preferred a smoother-textured cookie. So, I leave that up to you. These cookies work best if you use a homogenized peanut butter, rather than the natural varieties.

MAKES 24 TO 28 COOKIES

1¼ cups (188 g) unbleached all-purpose flour
¼ teaspoon baking soda
¼ teaspoon baking powder
¼ teaspoon fine salt
½ cup (113 g) unsalted butter, at room temperature
½ cup (110 g) packed dark brown sugar
½ cup (100 g) granulated sugar, plus ¼ cup (50 g) for dipping
½ cup (125 g) crunchy peanut butter
1 large egg
½ teaspoon vanilla extract
½ cup (75 g) roasted, salted peanuts, coarsely chopped (optional)
1 recipe Venezuelan Spiced Chocolate Ganache (page 27) or Hot Fudge Sauce (page 25)

Preheat the oven to 350°F (180°C). Line two large baking sheets with parchment paper and set them aside.

In a small bowl, mix together the flour, baking soda, baking powder, and salt with a wooden spoon. In the bowl of an electric mixer, cream the butter and sugars together until light and fluffy, about 3 minutes. Beat in the peanut butter, then add the egg and vanilla and beat until well blended. Beat in the dry ingredients, one-third at a time, until you have a soft dough. Then beat in the peanuts, if using, until they are well distributed.

Using a 1-tablespoon cookie scoop, place balls of dough 2 inches (5 cm) apart on the prepared baking sheets.

Place the remaining ¼ cup (50 g) of granulated sugar in a small, shallow dish. Moisten the bottom of a drinking glass with water, dip it in the sugar, then press the sugared bottom of the drinking glass into each cookie ball to flatten it, dipping the bottom of the glass in more sugar as needed. Bake the cookies on the upper and lower racks of the oven for 7 minutes, then switch the baking sheet positions. Bake for another 7 to 8 minutes or until the cookies are browned on the edges. Remove the cookies from the oven and let them cool completely on the baking sheets, about 30 minutes.

Dip half of each cookie into the warm chocolate ganache, then place the dipped cookies on wire racks to cool completely, about 30 minutes, before serving. Store the cookies in an airtight container at room temperature for up to 1 week.

Sour Cream Raisin Cookies

I'm not sure what magic happens in the oven, but the homely raisins in these bars taste like sultry chocolate after baking. I'm not kidding. A favorite in Minnesota and Wisconsin, these bar cookies are rich, moist, and delicious, and they can be portioned according to how many people you need to serve.

MAKES 8 TO 12 BARS

2	cups (328 g) raisins
1	cup (220 g) packed dark brown sugar
1¾	cups (157 g) old-fashioned rolled oats
1¾	cups (210 g) unbleached all-purpose flour
1	cup (227 g) unsalted butter, at room temperature
1	teaspoon baking soda
3	large egg yolks
1	cup (200 g) granulated sugar
1½	cups (375 ml) sour cream
2½	tablespoons cornstarch
1	teaspoon vanilla extract

Preheat the oven to 350°F (180°C).

In a small saucepan over medium heat, boil the raisins in 1 cup of water until plumped, about 5 minutes. Remove the pan from the heat, drain the raisins, and set them aside to cool.

In the bowl of an electric mixer, mix the brown sugar, oatmeal, flour, butter, and baking soda together until moist and crumbly. Pat half of the dough into a 13 x 9-inch (33 x 23-cm) baking pan.

Bake the dough for 7 minutes, then remove the pan from the oven.

Meanwhile, in a medium saucepan over medium heat, whisk together the egg yolks, sugar, sour cream, and cornstarch. Cook, whisking constantly, until the mixture thickens, about 10 minutes. Remove the saucepan from the heat, stir in the vanilla and the raisins, and pour the filling over the partially baked crust. Sprinkle the remaining unbaked dough on top of the filling and bake for 30 minutes, or until the top has browned. Remove the baking pan from the oven and let it cool completely before cutting into bars. Store them in an airtight container at room temperature for up to 3 days.

Chapter Five

TARTLETS, TARTS, PIES, and MORE

FOR SOME PEOPLE, PIE IS THE ANSWER to many of life's questions. More or less? Happy or sad? Together or solo? With the glide of a rolling pin, you decide on one crust or two, plain or fancy, and whether to share or keep it all to yourself.

Linda Hundt, owner of Sweetie-Licious Café and Bakery in the charming Michigan town of DeWitt, believes pie can change the world, simply by spreading goodwill. She calls rolling pins "the magic wands of our foremother pie bakers."

That's because pies and tarts are democratic common denominators. While cake usually means a special occasion, a good, homemade pie or tart is a friendly kind of dessert that welcomes all eaters. In many communities—especially in the South and Midwest—it's pie and coffee when neighbors come to call, when business people need to talk over a deal, or when friends gather to gossip. It's a slice of tart for ladies who lunch. Wedges of pie help raise funds at antique auctions, community events, and school functions. Turnovers, tartlets, and hand pies go with you to school, work, or on the road.

In this chapter, there are tartlets, turnovers, hand pies, crostatas, and pies to tempt all kinds of dessert lovers, whether they crave chocolate, cream, or fruit.

Pie used to be something that housewives made once a week, but all that has changed. These days, we roll out pastry much less often. Now, when we're faced with making a pie or tart for Thanksgiving or another special occasion, we forget the feel of the dough, the light touch we need to have. We tend to hurry the pastry along instead of giving it the time it needs.

That's why this chapter includes some pastries you can use right away and some that need more time. The easiest is the cream cheese dough in Miniature Toasted Pecan Tartlets in Cream Cheese Pastry (page 116), which you can virtually pat into the pan. The next in simplicity is the Sweet Almond Pastry (page 39) that you roll out between two pieces of parchment paper for a freeform tart with effortless cleanup, featured in Peach and Almond Crostata with Peach Leaf Whipped Cream (page 27) and Sweet Potato Crostata with Sugared Sage Leaves (page 130). Bougatsa (page 118), Greek custard tartlets, uses readymade filo dough; Golden Delicious Apple Tarts with Rosemary Caramel (page 120), Bistro-Style Tarte Tatin (page 136), and Blackberry and Lavender Turnovers (page 123) employ readymade puff pastry.

For the accomplished baker, the most challenging pastries include the buttery, shortbread-like dough for Luscious Lemon Meringue Pie (page 139) and the ultimate flaky pastry in Sparkly-Top Sour Cherry Pie (page 137). For those times when you need a good-tasting gluten-free option, Sweet Dumpling Tartlets with Maple Custard (page 121) use winter squash as their shells, and Vegan Chocolate Pie (page 142) really does taste like French Silk.

The *Bake Happy* baker makes a pie or tart in stages: the dough first, the filling next, and the topping last. The *really* savvy baker makes the pastry up to 3 months ahead of time and freezes it in discs, ready to thaw and use. Every recipe in this chapter contains tips and techniques to make the best version in the easiest and least stressful way, even if you only get your rolling pin out once a year.

Miniature Toasted Pecan Tartlets in Cream Cheese Pastry

Pecan pie is so ooey-gooey good, but it's also so rich that I prefer to eat it in small bites, as in these tartlets. If you're a novice pie baker, this is a great recipe to start with. For best results, the dough needs to be made and chilled before you're ready to bake. These tiny tartlets are great to have on hand for the holidays, weddings, or family reunions. They can be made ahead and kept for a week or so in an airtight container before baking.

MAKES 5 DOZEN TARTLETS OR 2 (8-INCH/20-CM) SINGLE-CRUST PIES

CREAM CHEESE PASTRY

1	cup (227 g) unsalted butter, at room temperature
2	(3-ounce/85-g) packages cream cheese, at room temperature
2	cups (250 g) unbleached all-purpose flour

FILLING

4	large eggs
3	cups (660 g) packed dark brown sugar
2	teaspoons vanilla extract
4	tablespoons unsalted butter, melted
⅛	teaspoon fine salt
2	cups (200 g) chopped pecans

For the pastry, in a food processor or in the bowl of an electric mixer, cream together the butter and cream cheese until smooth. Add in the flour and process or beat until a soft dough just comes together into a ball. Remove the dough from the food processor or bowl, wrap it in plastic wrap, and refrigerate it for 3 hours or overnight. Let the dough come to room temperature before using.

When you're ready to bake the pie, preheat the oven to 350°F (180°C).

For the filling, in the bowl of an electric mixer, beat the eggs until they are foamy and lightly lemon-colored, about 3 minutes. Beat in the brown sugar, vanilla, butter, and salt until you have a smooth filling. Set the filling aside.

When the dough comes to room temperature, divide it into four equal portions. Form each portion into 15 tablespoon-size balls. Press each ball into a mini-muffin cup to form the bottom and sides of each tartlet. Fill each tartlet with about 1 tablespoon of the filling and sprinkle the tops with the chopped pecans.

Bake for 25 to 30 minutes, or until the pastry has lightly browned and the filling has firmed. Remove the tartlets from the oven and let them cool for a few minutes in the pan before serving. Repeat with the remaining dough and filling.

○·················· **VARIATION** ··················○

TO MAKE A LARGE PECAN PIE, cut the dough in half instead of in quarters and press each portion into an 8-inch (20-cm) pie pan to form the crust. Divide the filling and pecans between the two pies. Bake for 40 to 45 minutes, or until the filling has firmed.

SO HAPPY TOGETHER

Pecans + Chocolate

To make these even more irresistible, drop a small piece of bittersweet chocolate into the middle of each tartlet before baking.

Bougatsa

There are ho-hum custard tarts—of the kind Lionel Hardcastle craves in the venerable British comedy "As Time Goes By"—and custard tarts that the rest of us could seriously crave. These tartlets consist of crackly, paper-thin pastry enclosing a sweet custard filling. To make the recipe, I combined a deep-dish custard known as galatoboureko from the Greek mainland with bougatsa from Crete, the best of both worlds. You can also take a cue from craft cocktails and make a fragrant Spice Syrup (page 28) to go with this, in place of the Orange Flower Honey Topping.

MAKES 16 TARTLETS

Unsalted butter, for the baking dish

CUSTARD FILLING

1	quart (1 L) half-and-half
1	teaspoon freshly grated orange zest
¼	teaspoon fine salt
⅓	cup plus 2 teaspoons (75g) granulated sugar
⅔	cup (100 g) dry farina breakfast cereal, such as Cream of Wheat
1	large egg
4	large egg yolks
1	teaspoon vanilla extract

PASTRY

12	(13 x 8½-inch/33 x 22-cm) sheets frozen filo pastry, thawed
½	cup (113 g) unsalted butter, melted

ORANGE FLOWER HONEY TOPPING

3	tablespoons amber honey, such as clover or wildflower
¼	teaspoon orange flower water
½	teaspoon ground cinnamon

Butter the inside of an 8- or 9-inch (20- or 23-cm) square baking dish and set it aside.

For the custard filling, bring the half-and-half, orange zest, and salt to a simmer in a large saucepan over medium-high heat. In a medium stainless-steel bowl, whisk together the sugar, farina, egg, and egg yolks; set it aside. Carefully and slowly, pour the hot milk into the farina mixture, whisking constantly. Transfer the mixture back to the saucepan and continue to cook over low heat, whisking constantly, until the custard becomes very thick, about 12 to 14 minutes. Whisk in the vanilla. Pour the custard into the prepared pan and set it aside to cool for 30 minutes, then cover the pan and refrigerate the custard for 3 hours or overnight.

When you're ready to bake the tartlets, preheat the oven 350°F (180°C). Line a baking sheet with parchment paper and set it aside.

Cut the chilled custard into 2-inch (5-cm) squares; don't worry if they are not perfectly firm.

For the pastry, place a sheet of filo pastry on a flat surface and brush it with some of the melted butter. Lay another sheet of filo on top and brush it with butter; repeat with a third and fourth sheet. With a pizza cutter or a small, sharp knife, cut the stacked sheets into six square-ish pieces. Arrange a square of custard in the center of each piece, on the diagonal, so there is a point of filo pastry on each side of the custard square. Fold the pastry over the custard like wrapping a present and place the tartlet, folded-side up, on the prepared baking sheet. Repeat the process with the remaining pastry and custard. Brush the top of each tartlet with any remaining melted butter.

Bake for 25 minutes or until the tartlets are golden brown. Remove the tartlets from the oven and let them cool on the baking sheet while you make the topping. For the topping, in a small bowl, stir together the honey and orange flower water. Drizzle each warm tartlet with the honey mixture and sprinkle with a little cinnamon before serving.

Serve warm or at room temperature. These are best enjoyed the same day they are made.

SO HAPPY TOGETHER

Honey + Orange Flower Water

I learned to make a brioche beehive cake from Natasha Goellner of Natasha's Mulberry & Mott bakery in Kansas City. The cake was delicious, but my big takeaway was the wonderful way that a few drops of orange flower water made the honey taste, well, honey-er. Bottled orange flower water, sometimes known as orange blossom water, is available online, at gourmet shops, and at Middle Eastern markets. Like any flower essence, a little goes a long way.

Golden Delicious Apple Tartlets with Rosemary Caramel

All the autumn delights of the first caramel apple reconfigure in this simple, homey dessert. Individual apple tartlets come out of the oven bubbly and sweet, and are then made even more luscious with homemade caramel sauce. Use Golden Delicious apples for their sweeter flavor, softer texture, and quick baking time. I prefer to use the all-butter Dufour or Trader Joe's puff pastry, available in the frozen food section.

MAKES 8 TARTLETS

1   (14-ounce/397-g or 16-ounce/454-g) package frozen puff pastry, thawed overnight in the refrigerator
8   Golden Delicious apples, peeled, cored, and very thinly sliced
8   teaspoons raw sugar, for sprinkling
4   tablespoons (60 g) unsalted butter, cut into small pieces
1   cup Rosemary Caramel (page 24) or prepared caramel sauce, warmed

Preheat the oven to 375°F (190°C). Line a baking sheet with parchment paper and set it aside.

Roll each sheet of pastry out on a lightly floured surface and cut out eight 6-inch/15-cm-diameter circles. Place the pastry circles on the prepared baking sheets. Arrange the apple slices in concentric rings on each pastry. Sprinkle each with a teaspoon of sugar and dot with a few pieces of butter.

Bake for 12 to 15 minutes or until the pastry is browned and cooked through and the apples have softened a little. Remove the tartlets from the oven and let them cool for a few minutes on the baking sheets. Drizzle each tartlet with Rosemary Caramel right before serving. These are best enjoyed the same day they are made.

"Good apple pies are a considerable part of our domestic happiness."

Jane Austen, in a letter to her sister Cassandra

Sweet Dumpling Tartlets with Maple Custard

A tart shell is meant to be sturdy enough to encase a filling during baking, yet attractive on its own. But who says a tart shell has to be pastry? If we like desserts that make their own sauces, then how about a vegetable that turns into a sweet tart, complete with its own shell? Sweet Dumpling squash, with their striped exterior and sunset-colored interior, are too beautiful to chop into oblivion, so let them be the star of the show. Boiling down the maple syrup first helps intensify its flavor in the custard filling. Serve the squash "tartlets" on dark green or brown dessert plates for the best effect—or line your white plates with autumn-colored cocktail napkins first.

MAKES 4 TARTLETS

½ cup (164 g) real maple syrup, preferably Grade B

4 rounded Sweet Dumpling squash, or acorn or other small winter squash

2¼ cups (550 ml) half-and-half

2 large egg yolks

1 large egg

¼ teaspoon fine salt

2 tablespoons gluten-free or other spice cookie crumbs, for garnish

In a small saucepan, bring the maple syrup to a boil over medium-high heat. Let the syrup cook until it reduces to 6 tablespoons, about 3 minutes. Remove the pan from the heat and set it aside.

Preheat the oven to 350°F (180°C). Line a 13 x 9-inch (33 x 23-cm) baking dish with parchment paper. With a sturdy knife, remove the top section of each squash so it stands about 2 inches tall; discard the top sections. With a spoon, remove and discard the seeds and stringy pulp from the inside of each squash. Place each cleaned squash shell in the prepared dish. Trim the bottoms, if necessary, so the squash sit evenly in the dish.

In a medium bowl, whisk together the half-and-half, egg yolks, egg, and salt until well blended. Whisk in the reduced maple syrup.

Divide the filling among the squash shells and bake for 1 hour and 15 minutes or until the tops of the squash are tender when pierced with a paring knife. Remove the dish from the oven and dust each squash "tartlet" with cookie crumbs. Serve hot or at room temperature, savoring each spoonful of crunchy topping, smooth custard, and tender squash.

Blackberry and Lavender Turnovers

With a package of puff pastry in the freezer and a jar of good blackberry jam, you can turn fresh blackberries with a hint of lavender into a summer treat. Pack up these turnovers for a summer concert on the lawn, a tasty reward after a hike, or a lunchbox goodie for day campers.

MAKES 8 TURNOVERS

1 sheet frozen puff pastry (from a 14-ounce/397-g or 16-ounce/454-g package), thawed overnight in the refrigerator

BLACKBERRY AND LAVENDER FILLING
½ cup (125 ml) blackberry jam
½ teaspoon organic, dried culinary-grade lavender buds
1½ cups (216 g) fresh blackberries
1 teaspoon freshly squeezed lemon juice

GLAZE
1 large egg, beaten
2 tablespoons granulated or raw sugar

SO HAPPY TOGETHER

Dark Berries + Lavender

A little sprinkle of dried lavender buds brings out the "purple" flavor in dark berries such as blackberries, blueberries, marionberries, and black raspberries.

Preheat the oven to 375°F (190°C). Line a large baking sheet with parchment paper and set it aside.

Place the puff pastry on a lightly floured surface and roll it out to a thickness of ¼ inch (6 cm). Using a pizza cutter or paring knife, cut the pastry into eight squares.

For the filling, combine the blackberry jam and lavender in a small saucepan over medium-high heat. Stir the mixture until the jam starts to bubble around the edges. Remove the pan from the heat and stir in blackberries and lemon juice.

To assemble the turnovers, brush the perimeter of each pastry square with a little water.

Spoon about ¼ cup (60 ml) of the filling into the center of each pastry square. Fold the squares in half on the diagonal to form a triangle. Press the edges together with the tines of a fork. Brush the top of each turnover with beaten egg and dust with sugar. With a paring knife, make three diagonal slits on top of each pastry. Place the turnovers on the prepared baking sheet.

Bake for 25 minutes or until the pastry is browned and the filling is bubbling. Remove the baking sheet from the oven and transfer the turnovers to a wire rack to cool. These are best enjoyed the same day they are made.

Strawberry-Rhubarb Hand Pies with Ballerina Sugar

On a visit to Portland, Oregon, I had the good fortune to visit Grand Central Bakery. They feature a different hand pie every season, made from local ingredients as much as possible. More flaky crust than filling, a good hand pie needs a more intensely flavored filling than a regular pie, such as this heady combination of strawberry and rhubarb. The pink ballerina sugar—think sparkly pink tutu—that tops these crispy pastries adds even more delight.

MAKES 9 HAND PIES

HAND PIE PASTRY

2	cups (250 g) unbleached all-purpose flour
1	tablespoon granulated sugar
1	teaspoon fine salt
1	cup (227 g) unsalted butter, chilled, cut into pieces
2	large eggs, divided
2	tablespoons whole milk

STRAWBERRY-RHUBARB FILLING

2	tablespoons water
2	cups (200 g) chopped fresh or frozen rhubarb, about 2 rhubarb stalks
1	cup (250 ml) strawberry preserves or jam
½	teaspoon rosewater

BALLERINA SUGAR

¼	cup (50 g) raw or turbinado sugar
	Red gel food coloring

For the Hand Pie Pastry, combine the flour, sugar, and salt in a food processor and pulse to blend. Add the butter pieces and pulse until the mixture resembles very coarse crumbs. Add one of the eggs and the milk and pulse just until the dough comes together. Remove the dough from the food processor and divide it in half. Press each half into a rough rectangle, wrap the rectangles in plastic wrap, and refrigerate for 1 hour.

For the Strawberry-Rhubarb Filling, combine the water and rhubarb in a medium saucepan over medium-high heat. Cook, stirring constantly, until the rhubarb has softened and breaks apart, about 5 minutes. Stir in the strawberry preserves and cook for 1 minute more. Remove the pan from the heat and stir in the rosewater. Set the filling aside to cool at room temperature.

For the Ballerina Sugar, place the sugar in a small bowl. Place a small dab of red gel food coloring on the end of a toothpick, and dip the toothpick into the center of the sugar. Remove the toothpick and mix the coloring into the sugar with a fork. Repeat this process until you achieve the shade of pink you want. Set the sugar aside.

Preheat the oven to 350°F (180°C). Line a large baking sheet with parchment paper and set it aside.

Remove the dough from the refrigerator, unwrap it, and place one of the pieces on a lightly floured work surface. Roll the dough out into a 9 x 12-inch (23 x 30-cm) rectangle. Trim the edges. Cut the rectangle into nine 3 x 4-inch (8 x 10-cm) rectangles. Repeat with the second piece of dough.

Place a generous tablespoon of filling in the center of nine of the rectangles. In a small bowl, beat the remaining egg with a fork, and brush the perimeter of the filled rectangles with the egg wash. Place another pastry rectangle on top, pressing along the perimeter with the tines of a fork to seal. Using a paring knife, cut a V-shaped vent in the top of each pastry.

Brush the tops of the pastries with the remaining egg wash and sprinkle with Ballerina Sugar.

Bake for 28 to 33 minutes or until the hand pies are golden brown. Remove the pies from the oven and let them cool on the baking sheet before serving. These are best enjoyed the same day they are made.

"Pumpkin pies, cranberry pies, huckleberry pies, cherry pies, green-currant pies, peach, pear, and plum pies, custard pies, apple pies, Marlborough-pudding pies,—pies with top crusts, and pies without…"

Harriet Beecher Stowe in *Oldtown Folks*, 1869

Peach and Almond Crostata with Peach Leaf Whipped Cream

After I lived, worked, and went to cooking school in Europe, I came back home to the Midwest with the fervor of a convert. My conversion, however, involved looking at Midwestern food in a new way, resulting in the James Beard-nominated Prairie Home Cooking, *which I'm happy to say has become a classic. After reading pioneer diaries, I was taken with using garden goodies like honeysuckle blossoms and peach leaves (organic) for flavoring. I still am. It's such a simple thing to do, but it really adds that extra, unexpected finish of complementary flavor. If you know someone with a peach tree, ask them to give you unsprayed peach leaves and go to town—or use a little almond extract instead. The easy dough—inspired by Australia's Donna Hay—rolls out to a large oval between two sheets of parchment paper, so there's no mess. You spread on the almond filling, then dot it with peaches, and slip it in the oven. You can do a "tavern cut" on this, as on long pizzas, using a pizza wheel or a mezzaluna. And I'll bet you can't eat just one piece.*

MAKES 1 (13 X 9-INCH/33 X 23-CM) TART

PEACH LEAF WHIPPED CREAM

16   fresh, organic peach leaves, stems removed, or substitute ½ teaspoon almond extract
1   cup (250 ml) heavy whipping cream
2   tablespoons granulated sugar

CROSTATA

½   cup (48 g) almond flour or finely ground almonds
¼   cup (50 g) granulated sugar
1   recipe Sweet Almond Pastry (page 39)
2½   pounds (1.25 kg) fresh peaches, peeled, pitted, and thinly sliced, about 5 cups

For the Peach Leaf Whipped Cream, combine the peach leaves and cream in a small saucepan over medium-high heat, and bring the cream to a boil. Remove the pan from the heat, cover, and let the mixture steep for 30 minutes at room temperature. Strain the cream through a fine-mesh sieve into an airtight container; discard the peach leaves. Let the cream cool to room temperature, then cover the container and refrigerate the cream until you're ready to use it, up to 2 days before serving. (If you are using almond extract instead of peach leaves, there's no need to steep the cream. Simply add the extract to the cream with the sugar before whipping.) Place the bowl of your electric mixer in the freezer to chill.

Preheat the oven to 350°F (180°C). Have two sheets of parchment paper and a large baking sheet ready.

For the filling, combine the almond flour and granulated sugar in a small bowl.

(recipe continues)

Place a sheet of parchment paper on a flat work surface. Transfer the Sweet Almond Pastry dough to the center of the parchment paper and form it into a 6-inch/15-cm-long cylinder. Place the second sheet of parchment paper over the dough and roll the dough into a large oval, roughly 13 x 9 inches (33 x 23 cm). Remove the top sheet of parchment paper. Transfer the pastry, still on the bottom piece of parchment paper, to the baking sheet. Scatter the almond and sugar mixture onto the dough, then scatter the peaches over top, leaving a 2-inch (5-cm) perimeter of dough. With your fingers, fold the perimeter of dough over the filling.

Bake for 27 to 30 minutes or until the pastry has browned and the filling in the center is firm to the touch.

Remove the crostata from the oven and let it cool on the baking sheet for 30 minutes. When the crostata is firm, transfer it to a serving platter.

To whip the cream, place the infused cream and sugar in the chilled bowl of an electric mixer fitted with the whip attachment and whip on high speed until thick, about 7 minutes. (If using almond extract, add it with the sugar.) Cut the crostata into pieces and serve each piece with a dollop of Peach Leaf Whipped Cream.

Berry Patch Tart

Fourth of July desserts—celebrating red, white, and blue—can look good but don't always taste that way. This year, let's declare our independence from ho-hum and go for woo-hoo instead! If you like, make the Fresh Herb Syrup (page 30) in advance—it also makes a great cocktail with the addition of a little vodka or gin and a squeeze of lime. Look for what berries are best and freshest in your garden, local U-pick farms, or the farmers' market.

MAKES 1 (13 X 9-INCH/33 X 23-CM) TART

1 recipe Sweet Almond Pastry (page 39)

12 ounces (340 g) strawberries, hulled and halved

12 ounces (340 g) whole blackberries, black raspberries, or blueberries

12 ounces (340 g) red raspberries

1 recipe Fresh Herb Syrup (page 30), prepared

1 (8.8-ounce/250-g) container mascarpone cheese

1 cup (250 ml) heavy whipping cream

Preheat the oven to 350°F (180°C). Have two sheets of parchment paper and a large baking sheet ready.

Place a sheet of parchment paper on a flat work surface. Transfer the Sweet Almond Pastry dough to the center of the parchment paper and form it into a 6-inch/15-cm-long cylinder. Place the second sheet of parchment paper over the dough and roll the dough into a large rectangle, roughly 13 x 9 inches (33 x 23 cm). Remove the top sheet of parchment paper. Transfer the pastry, still on the bottom piece of parchment paper, to the baking sheet.

Bake for 12 to 15 minutes or until the pastry has browned and is firm to the touch in the center.

Remove the baking sheet from the oven and let the pastry cool on the baking sheet for 30 minutes at room temperature. When the pastry is firm, transfer it to a serving platter.

For the filling, divide the berries into bowls, one type of berry to a bowl, and drizzle each bowl with 1 to 2 tablespoons of the Fresh Herb Syrup. Gently toss to coat the berries in the syrup.

For the filling, in the bowl of an electric mixer, whip together the mascarpone, 1 to 2 tablespoons of the Fresh Herb Syrup, and the heavy whipping cream until the mixture is light and fluffy, about 7 minutes. Spread the filling over the pastry.

Cut the tart into 12 small rectangles. Mound about ½ cup (125 ml) berries on top of each rectangle, so each rectangle has only one type of berry topping.

Serve the tart right away or cover it and refrigerate for up to 4 hours. This is best enjoyed the same day it is made.

Sweet Potato Crostata with Sugared Sage Leaves

With its beautiful fall colors, this freeform tart evokes autumn leaves, wood fires, and harvest home. What I also love about this tart is the fresh cider/citrus flavor that brings out the sweet potato. Too often, sweet potato dishes are buried in marshmallows or muddied with spices. The combination of cider syrup and coriander is light and bright. The crostata pastry can be rolled between two sheets of parchment paper, which keeps the mess at a minimum. If you like, prepare the Sugared Sage Leaves and cook the cider syrup and sweet potatoes a day ahead. You can also add freshly gathered autumn leaves from your own backyard to the Sugared Sage Leaves. I used golden linden and purplish-red Bradford pear leaves along with sage, scattered on top of the tart. If you wish to aromatize this tart after it has cooled, warm a little Spice Syrup (page 28) and drizzle it over each slice as you serve.

································· MAKES 1 (13 X 9-INCH/33 X 23-CM) TART ·································

SUGARED SAGE LEAVES

1	large egg white or 1½ teaspoons dried egg white mixed with 1½ tablespoons water
⅓	cup (67 g) granulated sugar
16	fresh sage leaves

SWEET POTATO CROSTATA

2	cups (500 ml) apple cider
¼	cup (50 g) granulated sugar
2	pounds (1 kg) sweet potatoes, about 4 large
2	large eggs
2	teaspoons ground coriander
⅛	teaspoon (a pinch) ancho chili powder
¼	teaspoon fine salt
1	recipe Sweet Almond Pastry (page 139), chilled

For the sugared sage leaves, in a small bowl, whisk the egg white until foamy. Place the sugar in another small, shallow bowl. Brush the leaves with the egg white, then dip them in the sugar. Place the sugared leaves on a wire rack and leave them to dry at room temperature for 2 to 3 hours. (You can also skip this step and just scatter fresh sage leaves on the tart as presentation, if you prefer.)

For the filling, stir the cider and sugar together in a small saucepan over medium-high heat, and bring the mixture to a boil. Cook for 20 minutes, stirring occasionally, or until the cider has reduced to ⅔ cup (158 ml), then remove the pan from the heat. Meanwhile, prick the sweet potatoes all over, using a paring knife, and microwave them on high for 12 minutes, or until they are soft when squeezed in the middle. Set the potatoes aside to cool for 10 minutes.

Wearing an oven mitt in one hand, slice each potato down the middle and scoop the cooked sweet potato pulp into a large bowl. With a potato masher, mash the sweet potatoes, then stir in the eggs, coriander, ancho chili powder, and salt until well blended. Stir in the cider syrup until well combined. Set the filling aside.

Preheat the oven to 350°F (180°C). Have two sheets of parchment paper and a large baking sheet ready.

Place a sheet of parchment paper on a flat work surface. Place the dough in the center of the parchment paper and form it into a 6-inch/15-cm-long cylinder. Place the second sheet of parchment paper over the dough and roll the dough into a large oval, roughly 13 x 9 inches (33 x 23 cm). Remove the top sheet of parchment paper. Transfer the pastry, still on the bottom piece of parchment paper, to the baking sheet.

Spoon the filling onto the dough, leaving a 2-inch perimeter, and smooth it out with a spatula. With your fingers, fold the perimeter of dough over the filling. Bake the crostata for 27 to 30 minutes or until the pastry has browned and the filling is firm to the touch in the center.

Remove the crostata from the oven and let it cool on the baking sheet for 30 minutes. When the crostata is firm, transfer it to a serving platter and scatter it with the Sugared Sage Leaves. Cut the crostata into pieces to serve.

SO HAPPY TOGETHER

Sweet Potato + Apple Cider

Sweet potato, so soft and mild, needs a little flavor contrast to be really interesting. Boiling apple cider until it reduces to a syrupy deliciousness results in a concentrated apple flavor that gives sweet potato an extra dimension.

Cinderella Pumpkin Tart with Toffee Glass Slippers

Everybody loves a Cinderella story. This tale of the persecuted heroine, transformed—can't we relate?—has popped up in 345 variants around the world, according to folklorists who count those things. The one we're most familiar with is the 1697 Charles Perrault tale with a fairy godmother, mice and birds that help out, and a pumpkin that turns into a carriage. The pumpkin of choice is a French heirloom, Rouge Vif d'Etampes, also known as the Cinderella pumpkin. Not only does this vivid orange, squatty pumpkin make for a good fairytale carriage, but it also makes an elegant tart with a couture color. To me, this tart compares to traditional pumpkin pie as a glass slipper compares to a garden clog. Look for this variety of pumpkin before Halloween, then keep it in a cool, dry place until you need it, or make the pumpkin purée right away. You will have more pumpkin purée than you need for one tart, but you can freeze it for up to 3 months and use it in Marbled Pumpkin Brownies (page 151) or other dishes calling for pumpkin purée. If you can't find a Cinderella pumpkin, simply wave your kitchen wand and turn a small sugar or pie pumpkin or a butternut squash into what you need. A scattering of clear toffee shards on the finished tart adds that final "dressmaker detail."

························ MAKES 1 (8-INCH/20-CM) TART ························

1	large Cinderella pumpkin
½	recipe Cinderella Pastry
½	cup (125 ml) clover or other amber honey
⅓	cup (66 g) granulated sugar
2	large eggs
½	cup (125 ml) heavy whipping cream
½	teaspoon ground cinnamon
½	teaspoon ground allspice
2	teaspoons freshly squeezed lemon juice
1	recipe Toffee Glass Slippers (page 37), prepared, or clear brittle candy

Preheat the oven to 375°F (190°C). Line a large baking sheet with aluminum foil.

For the filling, cut the pumpkin into eight pieces; remove and discard the seeds and stringy pulp. Place the pumpkin pieces on the prepared baking sheet. Bake for 45 minutes or until the pumpkin is tender when pierced with a fork. Remove the baking sheet from the oven and set it aside to cool.

When the pumpkin is cool enough to handle, scrape the pulp into a food processor; discard the rinds. Purée the pumpkin pulp until smooth. Set aside 2 cups (473 ml) for this recipe; cover and refrigerate the rest for up to 3 days or freeze it for up to 3 months. Wash and dry the food processor bowl.

Place the dough disc in the center of a sheet of parchment paper on a flat work surface. Place a second sheet of parchment paper over the dough and roll the dough out into a 10-inch (24-cm) circle. Remove the top sheet of parchment paper. Invert the pastry circle into an 8-inch (20-cm) round tart pan with a removable bottom; peel off the parchment paper and press the dough into the bottom and up the sides of the pan. Trim the edges by rolling a rolling pin over the rim of the tart pan, letting the excess pastry fall off, and prick the bottom of the pastry with the tines of a fork.

Preheat the oven to 325°F (160°C). Line the tart pan with parchment paper and fill it with dried beans or pie weights.

Bake the tart shell "blind" for 12 to 15 minutes or until lightly golden. Remove the pan from the oven. Remove the parchment paper and pie weights from the shell, and place the tart pan on a large baking sheet, keeping the oven on.

To finish the filling, place the puréed pumpkin in a medium mixing bowl. Pour the honey into a microwave-safe bowl and microwave it on high for 3 minutes or until the honey has reduced slightly and is a darker color. Add the honey to the pumpkin in the mixing bowl, along with the sugar, eggs, cream, spices, and lemon juice, and whisk the mixture until well blended. Pour the filling into the tart shell.

Transfer the tart, still on the baking sheet, to the oven. Bake for 40 to 45 minutes or until just set. Remove the tart from the oven and let it cool on the baking sheet for 30 minutes.

To serve, remove the sides of the tart pan and place the tart on a serving plate. Top with shards of Toffee Glass Slippers.

"The fine arts are five in number, namely: painting, sculpture, poetry, music, and architecture, the principal branch of the latter being pastry."

Antonin Carême (Marie-Antoine Carême), nineteenth-century food writer

Meyer Lemon and Pomegranate Tart

One of the delights of dark winter is that Meyer lemons and pomegranates are in season. Both shine in this dessert. The bright, aromatic Meyer Lemon Curd filling makes the little ruby slippers—pomegranate seeds—stand out. As delicious and colorful as this tart recipe is, however, it also makes a great template for other curd + fruit combinations. Try Blood Orange Curd (page 19) with Passion Fruit Blueberries (page 72), Lime Curd (page 20) with fresh raspberries, or Passion Fruit and Orange Curd (page 20) with fresh blackberries.

MAKES 1 (13¾ X 4¼ X 1-INCH/35 X 11 X 2.5-CM) TART

½   recipe Cinderella Pastry (page 38)

1   recipe Meyer Lemon Curd (page 20), prepared

1   (6-ounce/177-ml) container honeyed Greek yogurt, such as The Greek Gods brand

1   cup (250 ml) fresh pomegranate seeds

Unwrap the dough disc and place it in the center of a sheet of parchment paper on a flat work surface. Place a second sheet of parchment paper over the dough and roll the dough into a 16 x 6-inch (41 x 15-cm) rectangle. Remove the top sheet of parchment paper, and invert the dough into a 13¾ x 4¼ x 1-inch (35 x 11 x 2.5-cm) rectangular tart pan. Remove the parchment paper and press the dough into the bottom and up the sides of the pan. Trim the edges by rolling a rolling pin over the rim of the tart pan, letting the excess pastry fall off, and prick the bottom of the pastry with the tines of a fork. Refrigerate the formed dough for 30 minutes.

Preheat the oven to 325°F (160°C). Line the tart pan with parchment paper and fill it with dried beans or pie weights.

Bake the tart shell "blind" for 12 to 15 minutes or until it is lightly golden. Remove the pan from the oven. Remove the parchment paper and pie weights from the shell, let it cool to room temperature, about 30 minutes.

Loosen the pastry from the tart pan and transfer the shell to a serving platter. Spoon in the Meyer Lemon Curd and smooth the surface. Top with dollops of honeyed Greek yogurt and sprinkle with pomegranate seeds before serving.

Bistro-Style Tarte Tatin

When I went to cooking school in Paris, I would get up early every day to visit one of the many markets, then head to La Varenne in the eighth arrondissement for the hands-on morning class, where we prepared and then ate our lunch. The afternoon involved demonstration classes, where we would taste what the chefs had made. By early evening, I was ready for bistro food—hearty, unpretentious, and simple. That first taste of caramelized Tarte Tatin, the upside-down apple tart, was made all the more wonderful by a dollop of slightly sour crème fraîche. A heavy cast iron skillet is a must for this recipe. I also prefer to use puff pastry made with butter—from Dufour or Trader Joe's in the frozen food section—which takes about 2 hours to thaw at room temperature, or overnight in the refrigerator.

MAKES 1 (12-INCH/30-CM) TARTE TATIN

CRÈME FRAÎCHE

½ cup (125 ml) heavy whipping cream
½ cup (125 ml) sour cream

TARTE TATIN

6 tablespoons (90 g) unsalted butter
6 to 8 crisp apples, such as Gala, Jonagold, or Granny Smith, peeled, cored, and quartered
½ cup (100 g) granulated sugar
1 sheet frozen puff pastry (from a 14-ounce/397-g or a 16-ounce/454-g package), thawed overnight in the refrigerator

For the Crème Fraîche, in a medium bowl, whisk together the heavy whipping cream and sour cream until smooth. Cover the bowl and let it stand at room temperature for several hours or overnight. When it has thickened enough to spoon out and tastes slightly tart, serve it right away or cover it and refrigerate for up to 3 days.

Preheat the oven to 375°F (190°C). Roll out the puff pastry so that you can cut out a circle to fit just inside a deep, 12-inch (30-cm) cast iron skillet. Cover and chill the pastry in the refrigerator while you make the filling.

Melt the butter in a deep, 12-inch (30-cm) cast iron pan. Stir in the apples and sugar. Cook for about 20 minutes, stirring constantly to prevent the apples from sticking to the pan. Continue cooking for another 15 minutes or until the apples have caramelized and turned a deep, golden brown. Shake the pan from time to time to make sure the apples do not stick.

Place the chilled pastry over the apples in the pan.

Bake for 35 to 40 minutes or until the pastry is a deep, puffy, golden brown. Remove the pan from the oven and place a heatproof serving platter over the skillet. Using oven mitts, invert the skillet and give the bottom a firm tap to release any apples that may be sticking. Slowly release the skillet so the tart falls evenly onto the serving platter with its top crust now on the bottom. Cut the Tarte Tatin into wedges and serve it with dollops of Crème Fraîche.

Sparkly-Top Sour Cherry Pie

Cherries cheer you up. At least that's what songwriters had in mind when "Life Is Just a Bowl of Cherries" debuted in 1931 at the height of the Depression. A sour cherry pie with a sparkly top definitely does it for me. You can "officially" freeze a well-wrapped, unbaked fruit pie for up to 4 months, but I've frozen them for a year and then baked them from frozen with no discernible difference in taste. It's all in how well the pie is wrapped before freezing. Right before baking, brush milk over the top of the pie crust, then dust it with sugar for a sparkly top.

○⋯⋯⋯⋯⋯⋯⋯⋯⋯⋯⋯⋯⋯⋯ MAKES 1 (9-INCH/23-CM) PIE ⋯⋯⋯⋯⋯⋯⋯⋯⋯⋯⋯⋯⋯⋯○

FLAKY PIE PASTRY

2	cups (250 g) unbleached all-purpose flour
¼	teaspoon fine salt
½	teaspoon granulated sugar
3	tablespoons vegetable shortening or leaf lard, frozen and cut into small pieces
3	tablespoons unsalted butter, frozen and cut into small pieces
4	to 6 tablespoons ice water

SOUR CHERRY FILLING

24	ounces (750 g) pitted sour cherries, about 4 cups
1	cup (200 g) granulated sugar
3	tablespoons quick-cooking tapioca
1	tablespoon freshly squeezed lemon juice
1	teaspoon almond extract
1	tablespoon unsalted butter, cut into small pieces

SPARKLY TOPPING

2	tablespoons whole milk or heavy whipping cream
1	tablespoon sparkle sugar

For the pastry, combine the flour, salt, and sugar into the bowl of a food processor. Pulse to blend. Add the shortening and butter, and pulse quickly about ten times or until the mixture forms small crumbs. Drizzle 4 tablespoons of the ice water over the flour mixture. Pulse again several times or until the dough starts to form medium-size crumbs. Test the dough by trying to gather it into a ball with your hand. If you can gather it into a rough ball, stop pulsing. If the dough is still too crumbly, drizzle another tablespoon of ice water over the dough and pulse again to blend.

Transfer the dough to a lightly floured work surface. Gently gather the dough into a ball with your hands. Using the heel of your hand, press and smear one quarter of the dough about 6 inches (15 cm) across the surface. Repeat until all of the dough is smeared in the same direction. (This process creates layers that result in a flakier pastry.)

Using a dough scraper or pancake turner, gather the dough together into a rough cylinder. Cut the dough in half. Form each half into a ball, then flatten each ball slightly into a disc. Wrap each disc in plastic wrap and refrigerate for 30 minutes before rolling out (or wrap and freeze the dough for up to 6 months).

(recipe continues)

When you're ready to bake the pie, preheat the oven to 425°F (220°C). Have two pieces of parchment paper ready. Take one of the dough discs out of the refrigerator and place it in the center of one of the sheets of parchment paper. Place the second sheet of parchment paper over the dough and roll the dough into a 12-inch (30-cm) circle. Remove the top sheet of parchment paper. Transfer the pastry to a 9-inch (23-cm) pie plate and gently pat it in place. With a paring knife, trim the extra dough around the perimeter of the pie plate. Using the same method, roll out the remaining dough disc to a 12-inch (30-cm) circle and set it aside.

For the filling, in a large bowl, combine the sour cherries, sugar, tapioca, lemon juice, and almond extract. Fill the pastry shell with the sour cherry mixture. Dot the filling with the butter.

Moisten the edges of the bottom crust with a little water, then cover the filling with the top crust. Trim and flute the edges using the tines of a fork. Cut steam vents in the top crust. Brush the top with the milk or cream and sprinkle lightly with the sugar.

Place the pie on a baking sheet to catch any drips, and bake it for 15 minutes, then reduce the heat to 350°F (180°C) and bake for 45 to 60 minutes longer or until the crust is golden and juices are bubbling.

To bake a frozen pie, start at 450°F (230°C) for 15 minutes, then reduce the oven heat to 375°F (190°C) and bake for up to 60 minutes longer or until the filling is thickened and the crust is golden brown. Let cool, then cut into wedges and serve. Store any leftovers, lightly covered with aluminum foil, at room temperature for up to 2 days.

SO HAPPY TOGETHER

Sour Cherry + Almond

When I did a wheat harvest story for *Saveur* magazine, I interviewed descendants of the original Russian Mennonites who still made traditional dishes like sour cherry moos, a fruit soup featuring cherries cooked with the pits still in them for enhanced almond flavor. It turns out that bitter almonds and sour cherry pits contain the same flavor compound, benzaldehyde, so like all good flavor couples, they have something in common. Mahlab powder, made from the ground pits of wild Middle Eastern sour cherries, is used to flavor sweet doughs in Greece and the Middle East and has that same sour cherry and almond profile.

Luscious Lemon Meringue Pie

My love of lemon meringue pie is genetic. Both my grandmother and my mother had more lemon pie recipes than any other in their notebooks, scrapbooks, and recipe files. But we're not alone. According to a 2008 national survey by Schwan's Consumer Brands N. A., Lemon Meringue Pie was beloved by 24 percent of respondents, especially Midwesterners. So when I tasted a lemon meringue pie that was the best I had ever eaten, I begged the recipe from Megan Garrelts, the pastry chef who created it at Rye in Leawood, Kansas. I have adapted it here. The short-bread-like crust, the tart lemon filling, and the finish of torched, ethereal Swiss meringue that melts on the tongue all added up to the lemon meringue pie of my dreams. This recipe takes some skill and dedication—it's not something to attempt on short notice—but you can make the various parts a day ahead and put them together at the end. The egg wash on the crust helps keep it from getting soggy, and the Swiss Meringue will not weep as other meringues can. The pie will keep at room temperature or in the refrigerator for 24 hours—if it lasts that long.

○ ·········· ● MAKES 1 (9-INCH/23-CM) PIE ● ·········· ○

SINGLE-CRUST PASTRY

- 1 cup plus 2 tablespoons (105 g) all-purpose flour
- 1½ teaspoons granulated sugar
- ¼ teaspoon fine salt
- 4 tablespoons (57 g) unsalted butter, frozen and cut into small pieces
- 4 tablespoons (52 g) lard or vegetable shortening, frozen and cut into small pieces
- 3 to 4 tablespoons (45 to 40 ml) ice water
- 1 large egg, beaten

LUSCIOUS LEMON FILLING

- 6 large eggs
- 9 large egg yolks (6 of the whites will be used in the Swiss Meringue)
- 1 cup plus 2 tablespoons (225 g) granulated sugar
  Zest and juice of 6 lemons
- 18 tablespoons (270 g) unsalted butter
- 1 teaspoon fine salt
- 1 recipe Swiss Meringue (page 66)

(recipe continues)

For the Single-Crust Pastry, combine the flour, sugar, and salt in the bowl of a food processor bowl and set it in the freezer for 30 minutes along with the cubed butter and lard. Line a work surface with parchment paper or a silicone baking mat. Remove the food processor from the freezer, and pulse in the cold butter and lard until the mixture resembles pea-size crumbs. Slowly add 3 tablespoons of the ice water and pulse until the mixture is moist. Quickly transfer the dough to the prepared work surface. Gently gather the dough into a ball with your hand. Using the heel of your hand, press and smear one quarter of the dough about 6 inches (15 cm) across the surface. Repeat until all of the dough is smeared in the same direction. (This process creates layers that result in a flakier pastry.)

Using a dough scraper or pancake turner, gather the dough together. If the dough seems dry, sprinkle it with the remaining tablespoon of water and gather the dough together again. Then use the dough scraper to work the dough into a flat disc. You should still see butter flecks in the dough. Wrap and chill the dough disc for 30 minutes or up to 2 days. You can also wrap and freeze the dough for up to 3 months at this point; thaw it in the refrigerator before using.

For the Lemon Filling, in a medium, heavy-bottomed saucepan, whisk together the eggs, egg yolks, and sugar until smooth. Whisk in the lemon zest, lemon juice, butter, and salt, and place the pan over medium heat. Clip a candy thermometer to the inside of the pan and cook, whisking constantly, until the butter has melted completely and the mixture is foamy on top. Continue cooking for another 7 minutes; at this point the mixture should be thick enough to coat the back of a spoon, and it should register 160°F (75°C) on the candy thermometer. Remove the pan from the heat and let it stand for 5 minutes, then whisk the mixture again. Pass the filling through a fine-mesh sieve into an airtight container. Set the filling aside or cover the container and store it in the refrigerator for up to 3 days before using.

When you're ready to bake the pie, roll out the dough between two silicone mats or sheets of parchment paper to a rough 11-inch/28-cm-diameter circle. Line a 9-inch (23-cm) pie pan with the pastry, gently pressing the pastry into the bottom, up the sides, and a little bit over the edge of the pan. Trim the pastry around the perimeter of the pan. Use the tines of a fork to press a decorative border around the rim of pastry. Chill the pastry-lined pan in the freezer for 30 minutes.

Preheat the oven to 375°F (190°C). Line the pastry-lined pan with aluminum foil or a sheet of parchment paper and add pie weights or about 3 cups of dried beans. Blind-bake the crust for 20 minutes.

Remove the pan from the oven and set it on a heatproof work surface; carefully remove the foil or parchment and the weights. Reduce the oven heat to 350°F (180°C). Brush the bottom and sides of the pastry with the beaten egg wash.

Bake the pastry again for 10 minutes or until the egg wash has set.

Remove the pastry from the oven, but leave the oven on. Let the pastry cool for 10 minutes, then spoon in the filling.

Return the pie to the oven and bake for 15 to 20 minutes or until the filling has set and does not wobble when you gently shake the pie pan. Remove the pan from the oven and set it aside to cool for 30 minutes.

When you are ready to serve the pie, spoon or pipe the meringue over the filling. Using a hand-held kitchen torch, lightly toast the meringue, if you wish. Lemon meringue pie will keep at room temperature or can be covered and refrigerated for 1 day.

Pie + Plate

Does the type of dessert plate you choose really make a difference? Yes, conclude several research studies. Charles Spence and researchers from the Crossmodal Research Laboratory at Oxford University's Department of Experimental Psychology have shown how everything from the glass we drink out of to the color and shape of the plate we eat off of can influence our experience of what we consume. Serving a dessert on a round white plate will make it taste 10 percent sweeter than the same dessert served on a square black plate. We also tend to eat less of a dessert when it is in sharp color contrast to the plate. Megan Garrelts serves her Luscious Lemon Meringue Pie on a rustic, speckled plate that looks handmade ("Craft Collection" by Steelite) to emphasize the "Midwest food artisan" themes of the restaurant that she owns with her husband, Colby.

Vegan Chocolate Pie

My daughter Sarah, whose favorite pie is French Silk, makes this for her boyfriend's mother, who is vegan, and says you can hardly tell the difference. Serve it with fresh raspberries or strawberries.

MAKES 1 (9-INCH/23-CM) PIE

VEGAN CHOCOLATE WAFER CRUST

6½ ounces (190 g) dairy-free chocolate wafer cookies, crushed into fine crumbs

1 tablespoon maple or date sugar

3 ounces (90 g) vegan buttery stick (such as Earth Balance), melted and slightly cooled

VEGAN CHOCOLATE FILLING

13 ounces (400 g) dairy-free semisweet chocolate chips, (such as Ghirardelli: check the label)

⅓ cup (75 ml) strong brewed coffee

1 teaspoon vanilla extract

1 pound (454 g) silken tofu, drained

1 tablespoon real maple syrup, preferably Grade B

Preheat the oven to 350°F (180°C).

For the crust, in a medium bowl, stir together the cookie crumbs, sugar, and melted vegan buttery stick. Press this mixture firmly and evenly into the bottom, up the sides, and just over the lip of a 9-inch (23-cm) metal pie pan. Bake the crust on the middle rack of the oven until it is set and appears dry, 18 to 20 minutes. Remove the pan from the oven and let it cool completely at room temperature, about 1 hour.

For the filling, in a small saucepan or in the bottom of a double boiler, bring about 2 inches of water to a simmer over medium-high heat. In a medium metal mixing bowl or in the top of the double boiler, combine the chocolate chips, coffee, and vanilla. Set the bowl or top of the double boiler over the water, and stir the mixture with a spatula until the chocolate has melted.

In a blender or food processor, process the tofu, melted chocolate mixture, and maple syrup until smooth, about 1 minute. Pour the filling into the crust and refrigerate the pie for 2 hours or until the filling is firm. Serve immediately or cover and refrigerate the pie for up to 2 days.

Chapter Six

LITTLE CAKES, CUPCAKES, BROWNIES, and PASTRIES

F YOU'RE LOOKING FOR A CHARMING AND WHIMSICAL

way to serve dessert, why not forego the more formal layer cake in favor of little individual cakes? Little cakes guarantee more color, flavor, and fun with minimal decorating skills required. It's all in the cupcake liners, garnishes, and colored and flavored frostings, fillings, and icings.

A big part of the charm with little cakes and pastries is that you don't have to share. You can have one all to yourself, whether it is a Razzle-Dazzle Éclair (page 173) with raspberry icing, a Macaronette (page 148) that is easy to make, or a Lime Chiffon Cupcake with Blackberry Buttercream (page 160). Even when the little cake is cut from a bigger one, as in Gooey Butter Bars with Passion Fruit Blueberries (page 146) or Marbled Pumpkin Brownies (page 151), your little piece still looks and tastes special.

For even more delight, your little cake might have a secret filling, as in Coconut Lover's Cupcakes with Secret Filling (page 156) or Secret Filling Devil's Food Cupcakes (page 155). Or there could be a new interpretation of an old favorite, as in Citrus-Cardamom Twinkies (page 158) and Cherry Mashers, Pollock-Style (page 168), or the evocative Citrus and Browned Butter Madeleines with Burnt Honey Cream (page 153).

Good things come in small packages, when you're in *Bake Happy* world.

fluffy, then beat in the egg until blended. Alternate adding the flour and evaporated milk, beating until they are well incorporated. Add the corn syrup and vanilla and beat one last time until the batter is smooth. Pour the batter into the prepared crust.

Bake for 25 to 32 minutes, or until the cake is just nearly set. The top should remain moist and "gooey," so do be careful not to overbake it. Remove the cake from the oven and let it cool in the pan for a few minutes, then cut it into bars.

For the Passion Fruit Blueberries, gently toss the blueberries with the Passion Fruit Syrup in a medium bowl. Serve each Gooey Butter Bar topped with the blueberries. Store the bars at room temperature, covered, for up to 3 days.

Macaronettes

Move over, macaron! The method for these little cut-out cakes, sandwiched together with buttercream frosting, stream-lines the basics of macaron-making. As in macarons, the body of the macaronette is colorful but neutral in flavor; it's the filling that makes it pop, taste-wise. You simply spread the naturally gluten-free dacquoise batter in a pan, bake the cake, then cut it into circles. Spread the top of a cake circle with Easy Orange Buttercream Frosting, then sandwich it with another cake circle. And what better way to up the "happy factor" than with the color orange? I made these for my book club, and they were instantly gobbled up. The combination of moist, springy almond cake with fresh orange accents brings a smile. Moist and delicious, the dacquoise keeps for days covered on the kitchen counter and can be frozen for up to 6 months. Named for the town of Dax in southwestern France, this airy yet textured base can be piped from a pastry bag before baking or cut after baking to create many different shapes as well as the miniature trifles known as verrines. Change up the color and flavor of the dacquoise as well as the filling, and you can customize this recipe to suit your mood or any occasion.

MAKES 12 SANDWICH CAKES

Baking spray

DACQUOISE CAKE

8	large egg whites
¼	teaspoon fine salt
½	cup (100 g) granulated sugar
1	teaspoon almond extract
3¼	cups (300 g) almond flour or finely ground almonds
2¾	cups (300 g) confectioners' sugar, sifted
	Orange food coloring

EASY ORANGE BUTTERCREAM FROSTING

2	tablespoons unsalted butter, at room temperature
	Zest and juice of 1 orange
2	cups (240 g) confectioners' sugar, sifted

Preheat the oven to 350°F (180°C). Spray a 17 x 11-inch (43 x 28-cm) rimmed baking sheet with baking spray around the perimeter and diagonally. Place a sheet of parchment paper on top (the baking spray will help it stay in place).

For the Dacquoise Cake, in the bowl of an electric mixer, beat together the egg whites and salt until the mixture is just foamy, about 2 minutes, then increase the mixer speed to medium and beat until the egg whites turn white, about 4 minutes. Add the sugar, one-third at a time, continuing to beat on medium speed until soft peaks form, about 2 minutes more. Beat in the almond extract.

Combine the almond flour and confectioners' sugar in the bowl of a food processor and process the mixture into a fine powder. Using a rubber spatula and figure-8 strokes, fold the almond flour mixture into to the egg whites, one-third at a time. Continue folding until the batter is uniform in color.

To tint the batter, stir drops of orange food coloring into the batter until it reaches your desired shade.

Spoon the batter into the center of the prepared pan. Use an offset spatula to spread the batter to the edges of the pan and smooth the top. Wash and dry the bowl.

Bake for 12 to 15 minutes or until the cake has set, is pulling back from the edges of the pan, and springs back when you touch it in the center.

Remove the cake from the oven and carefully transfer it to a wire rack to cool for 30 minutes. Use the cake right away or wrap it in plastic wrap and keep it at room temperature for 2 days or in the freezer for up to 6 months.

For the Orange Buttercream Frosting, in the clean bowl of an electric mixer, beat together the butter, orange zest, orange juice, and confectioners' sugar until soft and creamy, about 3 minutes.

To assemble the macaronettes, use a 3-inch (7.5-cm) biscuit cutter to cut the cake into 24 circles. Spread a little filling on a cake circle, then top it with another circle. Repeat with the remaining cake circles and filling. Serve right away, piled on a cake stand. Store any leftovers in an airtight container at room temperature for up to 3 days.

VARIATIONS

FOR PISTACHIO-CARDAMOM DACQUOISE, in place of almond flour, grind 10 ounces (300 g) roasted, shelled, unsalted pistachios in the food processor until you have a fine-grained pistachio flour. Add the confectioners' sugar and 1 teaspoon of ground cardamom and continue with the recipe. For Pistachio Filling, substitute whole milk for the orange juice, plus ½ teaspoon almond extract and a little green food coloring.

FOR HAZELNUT-CHOCOLATE DACQUOISE, omit the almond extract. In place of almond flour, grind 10 ounces (300 grams) whole, raw, skin-on hazelnuts in the food processor until you have a fine-grained hazelnut flour. Add ¼ cup cocoa powder to the hazelnut flour, and continue with the recipe. Use a chocolate hazelnut spread such as Nutella for the filling.

SO HAPPY TOGETHER

Hazelnut + Chocolate

Hazelnut and chocolate, writes Niki Segnit in *The Flavor Thesaurus*, is a "heavenly combination" that owes its inspiration to a chocolate shortage in late-nineteenth-century Italy, when chocolate had to be bulked up with ground hazelnuts to make it go farther. By 1951, the combination was sold in a jar as a spread known as Supercrema Gianduja. In 1964, the name was changed to Nutella.

VA-VA-VOOM VERRINES

Verrines, from the French word for glass, are small, miniature desserts served in tiny glass or plastic containers. Very French, très chic. They look like tiny English trifles, layered with cake, colorful filling, a cloud of topping, and a sprinkle of something fun to finish them off. Verrines are a great way to do dessert for a buffet or a gathering. First, you find the type of glass you want at a party supply store: square, rectangular, round, or boat-shaped. Then make and have ready the components: the dacquoise from Macaronettes (page 148), a flavored Pastry Cream (page 22) or fruit curd (page 19), a cloud of whipped cream or honeyed Greek yogurt, and Homemade Colored Sprinkles (page 35) or chopped nuts or sparkly sugar.

To assemble the verrines, you simply cut the dacquoise to fit in the bottom of each little container, then dollop on the filling, or pipe it from a pastry bag. Sprinkle on the topping, and voilà!

Marbled Pumpkin Brownies

These moist and delicious brownies are good any time of year, but especially in the fall, when you start to crave the flavors of pumpkin and spice. It's easy to marble these brownies to look like fine, handmade Florentine paper—just as beautiful to look at as they are to eat. If you like, serve these garnished with Sugared Sage Leaves (page 130).

···················· **MAKES 25 TO 30 BROWNIES** ····················

Baking spray

PUMPKIN BROWNIE BATTER

2 cups (500 g) granulated sugar

3 cups (285 g) unbleached all-purpose flour

1 tablespoon baking powder

1 tablespoon baking soda

1 tablespoon ground cinnamon

¾ teaspoon fine salt

1½ cups (375 ml) canola oil

2 (15-ounce/425-g) cans unsweetened pumpkin purée

4 large eggs, lightly beaten

1 cup chopped pecans, dried cherries, or raisins (optional)

CREAM CHEESE MARBLING

2 (8-ounce/226-g) packages cream cheese, at room temperature

¾ cup (160 g) granulated sugar

2 teaspoons vanilla extract

¼ cup (60 ml) heavy whipping cream

2 large eggs

Preheat the oven to 325°F (160°C). Spray a 13 x 9-inch (33 x 23-cm) pan with baking spray and set it aside.

In a large bowl, combine the sugar, flour, baking powder, baking soda, cinnamon, and salt. Add the oil and beat with an electric mixer until the dry ingredients are just moistened. Beat in the pumpkin until smooth, then beat in the eggs for 1 minute. Fold in the nuts, cherries, or raisins, if using.

For the Cream Cheese Marbling, in a medium bowl, beat together the cream cheese and sugar with an electric mixer. Beat in the vanilla, cream, and eggs until smooth.

Pour half of the pumpkin batter into the prepared pan. Pour the marbling over the pumpkin batter, then spoon the remaining pumpkin batter on top. Using a table knife, swirl the two together to create a pleasing pattern.

Bake for 40 to 45 minutes, or until a cake tester inserted in the center comes out clean. Remove the brownie pan from the oven and let cool for 30 minutes, then cut into squares to serve. Store the brownies, covered, at room temperature for up to 3 days.

Citrus and Browned Butter Madeleines with Burnt Honey Cream

If there ever were a mindful thing to bake, it is madeleines. These little cakes can be tricky—you'll need a madeleine pan—so set aside the time, follow the directions, and give yourself up to the moment and the exacting method. I've found that lightly but thoroughly coating the madeleine molds with baking spray—definitely not French, but it works— is the easiest way to get the scallop shell-shaped cakes out of the molds after baking. Only fill the madeleine molds halfway. Just figure that the first batch is practice, and they don't have to be perfect, just delicious. You'll be rewarded with the scent and flavor of citrus and browned butter in the madeleines and caramelized honey in the dipping sauce. You'll be transported to a happy place, just as Proust was in his early-twentieth-century novel In Search of Lost Time. *When I make madeleines, I'm back at Dehillerin in Paris, an Aladdin's cave of culinary equipment, where I bought my madeleine pan while studying at La Varenne Ecole de Cuisine. Adapted from a recipe by Eryn Chesney.*

MAKES 24 LARGE OR 40 SMALL MADELEINES

CITRUS AND BROWNED BUTTER MADELEINES

½ cup (113 g) unsalted butter, plus more for the pan

3 large eggs, at room temperature

⅔ cup (130 g) granulated sugar

1 cup (125 g) unbleached all-purpose flour, plus more for the pan

1 teaspoon vanilla extract

½ teaspoon freshly grated lemon zest

½ teaspoon freshly grated orange zest

½ teaspoon baking powder

Baking spray

Confectioners' sugar, for dusting

BURNT HONEY CREAM

½ cup (170 g) clover, wildflower, or other amber honey

1½ cups (375 ml) heavy whipping cream

⅛ teaspoon fine salt

For the Citrus and Browned Butter Madeleines, melt the butter in a small light-colored or stainless steel skillet over medium-high heat until it turns a golden brown. The butter will foam, then the foam will subside; bigger, clear bubbles will form, and in about 1 to 2 minutes from that point, the butter will start to brown. Remove the pan from the heat and let the butter cool until it is just warm.

In the bowl of an electric mixer, beat the eggs and sugar together until the mixture is thick and pale yellow. The mixture

(recipe continues)

should ribbon from the beaters when you stop the mixer and lift the beaters up. With a spatula, fold in the flour, vanilla, citrus zests, and baking powder until smooth and well blended. Fold in the browned butter, including the browned bits from the bottom of the pan, until well blended. Cover and refrigerate the batter for at least 1 hour or overnight.

When you're ready to bake the madeleines, preheat the oven to 375°F (190°C). Lightly but thoroughly spray the inside of a madeleine pan with baking spray; wipe out any extra baking spray foam with a paper towel, as this could interfere with the scallop shell design. Fill each cavity half full with batter. The batter will spread and fill each mold as it bakes.

Bake for 8 to 10 minutes or until the edges of the cakes turn golden brown and the tops feel springy to the touch. Remove the pan from the oven and turn the madeleines out of the pan onto wire racks, using a table knife to help dislodge them, if necessary. Dust the warm madeleines with confectioners' sugar.

Respray the madeleine pan and repeat the process with the remaining batter.

For the Burnt Honey Cream, bring the honey to a boil in a small saucepan over medium-high heat. Cook until the honey has caramelized and reduced slightly, about 4 minutes. Carefully whisk in the cream until it is well blended and continue to cook over medium-high heat until the cream has thickened enough to coat the back of a spoon. Stir in the salt, remove the pan from the heat, and set the sauce aside to cool.

To serve, dip the madeleines in the burnt honey cream, sip your tea, and wander back in time. Madeleines are best enjoyed the same day they are made.

Secret Filling Devil's Food Cupcakes

Everyone from Girl Scouts to dinner guests will love these cupcakes with the secret filling baked inside. They bring out the kid in all of us. Chocolate Ganache (page 27) or Cocoa Frosting (page 167) spread over these cooled cupcakes will have chocoholics swooning.

○·· MAKES 30 CUPCAKES ··○

SECRET CREAM FILLING

1	(8-ounce/226-g) package cream cheese, at room temperature
1	large egg, beaten
½	teaspoon fine salt
⅓	cup (67 g) granulated or raw sugar

DEVIL'S FOOD CAKE

3	cups (285 g) unbleached all-purpose flour
2	cups (500 g) granulated or raw sugar
1	teaspoon fine salt
½	cup (60 g) unsweetened cocoa powder
2	teaspoons baking soda
2	cups (500 ml) hot water
2	teaspoons cider vinegar
2	teaspoons vanilla extract
⅔	cup (150 ml) vegetable oil

FROSTING

Chocolate Ganache (page 27) or Cocoa Frosting (page 167), prepared and cooled

Preheat the oven to 350°F (180°C). Line three standard 12-cup cupcake pans with 30 paper liners and set them aside.

For the Secret Cream Filling, in the bowl of an electric mixer, beat the cream cheese until smooth and fluffy, about 2 minutes. Beat in the egg, salt, and sugar. Set the filling aside.

For the Devil's Food Cake, in a large bowl, combine the flour, sugar, salt, and cocoa powder. In a separate medium bowl, mix together the baking soda and hot water, then stir in the vinegar, vanilla, and oil. Pour this mixture into the dry ingredients and mix with a wooden spoon until the batter is smooth and evenly colored.

Fill each cupcake liner half full with batter. Spoon a large tablespoon of filling on top of the batter in each cupcake liner. Divide the remaining cake batter among the cupcake liners, covering the filling.

Bake for 20 to 25 minutes, or until a toothpick inserted in the center of a cupcake comes out clean.

Remove the cupcakes from the oven and let them cool completely in the pans. Frost the cupcakes with cooled Chocolate Ganache or Cocoa Frosting and serve. Store the cupcakes at room temperature for up to 3 days.

Coconut Lover's Cupcakes with Secret Filling

Who doesn't like a secret filling? Especially one hidden in a cloud-like cupcake snowy with coconut? This easy yellow cake gets extra flavor from coconut milk creamer (I used the So Delicious brand) infused with sweetened flaked coconut. Change up the filling based on what you have on hand or what you're craving—room temperature Chocolate Ganache (page 27) or Hot Fudge Sauce (page 25), any of the fruit curds (page 19), Sea Salt Caramel (page 24), good-quality fruit preserves, or extra Coconut Frosting. You can find coconut creamer in the refrigerated health section of the grocery store.

○ · MAKES 24 CUPCAKES · ○

COCONUT LOVER'S CAKE

1	cup (100 g) sweetened flaked coconut
1½	cups (350 ml) coconut milk creamer
1	teaspoon coconut extract
2	cups (250 g) unbleached all-purpose flour, sifted
½	cup (100 g) granulated sugar
1	tablespoon baking powder
1	teaspoon fine salt
½	cup (113 g) unsalted butter, at room temperature
1	teaspoon vanilla extract
2	large eggs

SECRET FILLING

1	recipe Chocolate Ganache (page 27) or any of the fruit curds (pages 19–20), prepared

SEVEN-MINUTE FROSTING

1½	cups (300 g) granulated sugar
2	large egg whites
5	tablespoons (70 ml) water
1	tablespoon light corn syrup
¼	teaspoon fine salt
1	teaspoon vanilla extract
	Sweetened flaked coconut, for garnish

For the Coconut Lover's Cake, combine the sweetened flaked coconut and coconut milk creamer in a 4-cup (1-L) microwave-safe measuring cup. Microwave on high for 2 minutes, then cover the measuring cup and let the mixture infuse at room temperature for 30 minutes (this can be done up to 2 days ahead). Stir in the coconut extract.

When you're ready to bake the cupcakes, preheat the oven to 350°F (180°C). Line two standard 12-cup cupcake pans with paper liners and set them aside.

Sift the flour (again), sugar, baking powder, and salt into the bowl of an electric mixer. Add the butter, vanilla, eggs, and infused coconut milk creamer. Beat the mixture on medium speed for 3 to 4 minutes, scraping down the sides of the bowl, until the batter is smooth.

Fill each cupcake liner halfway full with batter.

Bake for 16 to 18 minutes, or until a toothpick inserted in the center of a cupcake comes out clean. Remove the cupcakes from the oven and let them cool in the pans for 30 minutes.

Using a cupcake corer, a serrated steak knife, or a grapefruit spoon, cut out a small core in the center of each cupcake and save the cut out cake for another use, such as a treat for the baker or Verrines on page 150 (wrap and freeze the excess cake for up to 3 months). Spoon about 1 to 2 teaspoons of filling in each core. Set the cupcakes aside.

For the Seven-Minute Frosting, in a small saucepan or in the bottom of a double boiler, bring about 2 inches of water to a simmer over medium-high heat. In a medium metal mixing bowl or in the top of the double boiler, combine the sugar, egg whites, water, corn syrup, and salt. Set the bowl or top of the double boiler over the water. Using a hand-held mixer, beat the mixture on high speed for 5 to 7 minutes, or until the frosting turns a bright white and triples in volume. Beat in the vanilla and remove the bowl or double boiler from the heat. Use the frosting right away or cover it and refrigerate for up to 1 day. Let the frosting come to room temperature before using.

Frost each cupcake with Seven-Minute Frosting and garnish with sweetened, flaked coconut. Store the cupcakes uncovered at room temperature for up to 3 days.

SO HAPPY TOGETHER

Wisteria + Sunshine

In Elizabeth von Arnim's classic *The Enchanted April*, two women plan and scrimp and save after they read an ad in a London newspaper: "To Those Who Appreciate Wisteria and Sunshine." They want a one-month vacation from rainy, cold London life, including their marriages, which had gotten stuck in different ruts. With two other companions, they book San Salvatore, a castello in Portofino, with views toward Genoa on one side and the mountains on another. This unstructured, sunny time to do whatever they like restores and renews them. Lotty Wilkins is the first to feel that power. The first morning at the castello, she opens her window and feels the breeze, watches boats out on the bay, smells the scents of the garden. "Happy?" von Arnim writes of Lotty. "Poor, ordinary, everyday word. But what could one say, how could one describe it? It was as though she could hardly stay inside herself, it was as though she were too small to hold so much of joy, it was as though she were washed through with light."

Citrus-Cardamom Twinkies

People were in a panic when Hostess Twinkies suddenly disappeared from grocery store shelves in 2013. Twinkies debuted in 1930 with a banana cream filling that was switched to vanilla after World War II. I loved Twinkies as a kid, but as an adult, I want more flavor and better ingredients. I came across Alison Okabayashi of Pretty Please Bakery in San Francisco who creates her own versions, which she calls "Twinks," in upscale flavors of red velvet, pumpkin, and raspberry. They're part of her "Nostalgics" line that also includes Ding Dongs and Whoopie Pies. Inspired by Alison's creations, these Twinkies deliver on flavor with an orange glaze, a tender citrus-scented chiffon cake, and a fluffy filling. I had one wrapped up to give to a friend, but during a bad patch of cold winter weather, I forgot it in the back seat of my car for a week. When I unwrapped it and took a bite, just to see, it was still moist and delicious in true—but preservative-free—Twinkie style. To make these nostalgic treats, you'll need a canoe or Twinkie pan, which you can find at craft stores, cake supply shops, or online.

○ ⋯⋯⋯⋯⋯⋯⋯⋯⋯⋯⋯⋯ MAKES 18 TWINKIES ⋯⋯⋯⋯⋯⋯⋯⋯⋯⋯⋯⋯ ○

Baking spray, for the pan

TWINKIE CHIFFON CAKE

4	large egg whites
¼	teaspoon cream of tartar
1	cup plus 2 tablespoons (108 g) cake flour
¾	cup (160 g) granulated sugar
1½	teaspoons baking powder
½	teaspoon fine salt
⅓	cup (75 ml) cold water
¼	cup (59 ml) vegetable oil
1½	teaspoons freshly grated lemon zest
	Juice of 1 lemon
3	large egg yolks

MARSHMALLOW FILLING

6	tablespoons (90 g) unsalted butter, at room temperature
1	cup (120 g) confectioners' sugar, sifted
2½	teaspoons vanilla extract
⅛	teaspoon fine salt
1	(7-ounce/198-g) jar marshmallow crème

GLAZE

1	recipe Orange-Cardamom Syrup (page 32)

Preheat the oven to 325°F (160°C). Spray the inside of a canoe or Twinkie pan with baking spray and set it aside.

For the Twinkie Chiffon Cake, in the bowl of an electric mixer, beat the egg whites with the cream of tartar almost until stiff peaks form—the peak should just turn over as you remove the beaters, about 6 minutes; set the bowl aside. In another large bowl, sift together the flour, sugar, baking powder, and salt; set the bowl aside. In a separate small bowl, stir together the cold water, oil, lemon zest and juice, and egg yolks, and stir this mixture into the dry ingredients to make a smooth batter.

Pour the batter over the beaten egg whites, one-third at a time, folding the batter into the egg whites with a rubber spatula, using a figure-8 pattern and scooping up from the bottom of the bowl until the batter is evenly colored. Fill each cylindrical depression in the canoe pan half full with batter.

Bake until the tops of the cakes spring back when lightly touched and are a golden color, about 15 minutes. Remove the pan from the oven and turn the cakes out onto a cooling rack. Re-spray the canoe pan and repeat the process with the remaining batter. Let the Twinkies cool completely after baking.

For the Marshmallow Filling, in the bowl of a food processor or electric mixer, combine the butter, confectioners' sugar, vanilla, salt, and marshmallow crème and process or beat the mixture until smooth.

To assemble the Twinkies, cut each one almost in half lengthwise, like you would a hot dog bun. Spread about 1 to 2 tablespoons of filling on the bottom half and sandwich the top and bottom halves together. Place each filled Twinkie on a sheet of aluminum foil or parchment paper for easier cleanup. Brush each one with the glaze and let them sit for 30 minutes to dry. Serve the Twinkies right away or store them in an airtight container at room temperature for up to 1 week.

Lime Chiffon Cupcakes with Blackberry Buttercream

Violet and chartreuse sit just far enough away from each other on the color wheel to be an interesting combination. Likewise, blackberry and lime might not be a flavor combination that immediately springs to mind, but it's delicious, like a blackberry margarita. Use the leftover egg yolk when you scramble eggs the next morning.

MAKES 18 CUPCAKES

LIME CHIFFON CAKE

4	large egg whites
¼	teaspoon cream of tartar
1	cup plus 2 tablespoons (108 g) cake flour
¾	cup (160 g) granulated sugar
1½	teaspoons baking powder
½	teaspoon fine salt
⅓	cup (75 ml) cold water
¼	cup (60 ml) vegetable oil
1	teaspoon freshly grated lime zest
	Juice of 1 lime
3	large egg yolks

BLACKBERRY BUTTERCREAM

½	cup (113 g) unsalted butter, at room temperature
½	cup (120 g) fresh blackberries, rinsed and patted very dry
1	teaspoon vanilla extract
½	teaspoon freshly grated lime zest
⅛	teaspoon fine salt
1	(16-ounce/454-g) package plus 1 cup (120 g) confectioners' sugar, sifted

Preheat the oven to 325°F (160°C). Line two standard cupcake pans with 18 liners and set them aside.

For the Lime Chiffon Cake, in the bowl of an electric mixer, beat the egg whites with the cream of tartar until almost stiff peaks form—the peak should just turn over as you remove the beaters; set the bowl aside. In another large bowl, sift together the flour, sugar, baking powder, and salt; set the bowl aside. In a separate small bowl, stir together the cold water, oil, lime zest and juice, and egg yolks, then stir this mixture into the dry ingredients to make a smooth batter.

Pour the batter over the beaten egg whites, one-third at a time, folding the batter into the egg whites with a rubber spatula, using a figure-8 pattern and scooping up from the bottom of the bowl until the batter is evenly colored. Fill each cupcake liner half full with batter.

Bake until the tops of the cupcakes spring back when lightly touched and are a golden color, about 15 minutes. Remove the cupcakes from the oven and let them cool completely in the pan before frosting.

For the Blackberry Buttercream, in the clean bowl of an electric mixer, combine the butter, blackberries, vanilla, lime zest, and salt and beat until the mixture is creamy. Add the confectioners' sugar, 1 cup at a time, beating on low speed after each addition until the buttercream is blended and smooth.

If you like, scoop the frosting into a piping bag fitted with a star tip and pipe the buttercream on each cupcake, or simply frost each cupcake with a spatula. Store the cupcakes at room temperature for up to 3 days.

SO HAPPY TOGETHER

Blackberry + Lime

Blackberries, like grapes, take on the flavor of their terroir or micro-climate and growing conditions. That's why blackberries picked in the wild are oh so much more interesting that those you buy at the grocery store. They may have floral or cedar or wine notes, while their tamer cousins taste of sweet "nice girl" fruit. Wild blackberries pair well with the dependable flavor of apple, but the more modest cultivated blackberries can be livened up by a walk on the wild side with bad-boy lime.

Carrot, Zucchini, and Yellow Squash Cupcakes

Lots of people love carrot cake. But for the baker, making the same recipe over and over and over again can start to feel a little, well, ho-hum. This fresh spin on a classic features grated and spiced carrots, zucchini, and yellow squash. Use small, trimmed zucchini and yellow squash and grate them whole. If you like, spoon the batter into cupcake liners in complementary colors. Traditional cream cheese frosting and vegetable garden confetti are the crowning glories.

····· MAKES 36 CUPCAKES ·····

CUPCAKES

6	large eggs, at room temperature
3	cups (603 g) granulated or raw sugar
2	cups (500 ml) canola oil
3¾	cups (585 g) unbleached all-purpose flour
1	tablespoon baking soda
1	tablespoon baking powder
1½	teaspoons fine salt
1½	cups (192 g) grated zucchini, from about 3 small
1½	cups (192 g) grated yellow summer squash, from about 3 small
1½	cups (192 g) grated carrot, from about 4 large
1	teaspoon ground coriander
1	teaspoon ground cinnamon
1	teaspoon ground ginger
1½	cups (250 g) raisins
1½	cups (222 g) chopped pecans or walnuts

VEGETABLE GARDEN CONFETTI

½	cup (60 g) grated zucchini
½	cup (60 g) grated yellow squash
½	cup (60 g) grated carrots
¼	cup (50 g) granulated sugar
2	tablespoons water
1	teaspoon freshly grated lemon zest

CREAM CHEESE FROSTING

2	(8-ounce/226-g) packages cream cheese, at room temperature
5	tablespoons (74 g) unsalted butter, at room temperature
5	cups (600 g) confectioners' sugar, sifted
1	tablespoon vanilla extract

Preheat the oven to 350°F (180°C). Line three standard 12-cup cupcake pans with liners, and line a small baking sheet with parchment paper; set the pans aside.

In the bowl of an electric mixer, beat the eggs with the sugar until the mixture is light and frothy, about 3 minutes. Beat in the oil. In a separate large bowl, sift together the flour, baking soda, baking powder, and salt. Add the dry ingredients to the egg mixture, 1 cup at a time, beating well after each addition. Using a wooden spoon or spatula, stir in the grated vegetables, coriander, cinnamon, and ginger until well blended, then fold in the raisins and nuts. Fill the cupcake liners three-quarters full with the batter. Wash and dry the batter bowl.

Bake for 20 to 25 minutes, or until a cake tester inserted in the center of a cupcake comes out clean. Remove the cupcakes from the oven and let them cool completely in the pans. Reduce the oven temperature to 225°F (110°C).

For the Vegetable Garden Confetti garnish, combine the grated vegetables, sugar, water, and lemon zest in a saucepan over medium-high heat. Cook, stirring, until the vegetables are translucent and resemble candied confetti, about 8 to 10 minutes. Spread the confetti in a thin layer on the prepared baking sheet and bake it until crisp and dry to the touch, about 30 minutes. Remove the confetti from the oven and set it aside to cool on the baking sheet.

For the Cream Cheese Frosting, in the bowl of an electric mixer, beat together the cream cheese and butter until the mixture is light and fluffy, about 4 minutes. Add the sugar and vanilla and beat until smooth.

Frost the cupcakes after they have cooled and while the frosting is soft and spreadable. When the vegetable confetti is cool enough to handle, sprinkle it on the top of the frosted cupcakes and serve. Store the cupcakes at room temperature for up to 3 days.

"Vegetables are a must on a diet. I suggest carrot cake, zucchini bread, and pumpkin pie."

Jim Davis, cartoonist and creator of *Garfield*

Chai Cupcakes

These all-natural, linen-colored cupcakes are also vegan and gluten-free. Baking them in unbleached cupcake papers continues the color and ingredient theme. When I was shopping for the chai spices in an Indian/Pakistani grocery store in my neighborhood, I found something else in the spice aisle—a jar of multi-colored fennel, sesame, and coriander seeds, known as mukhwas, *that function as after-dinner mints. They worked great as colored sprinkles and as a bed on which I nestled the cupcakes for an easy presentation. For the best flavor, I ground the cardamom in a spice grinder and grated fresh nutmeg with a microplane grater. I used a pastry bag fitted with a star tip to pipe the frosting onto the gently spicy cupcakes.*

MAKES 14 CUPCAKES

CHAI CUPCAKES

¾ cup (175 ml) boiling water

1 chai tea bag

1¾ cups (165 g) gluten-free unbleached all-purpose flour

1 teaspoon ground cinnamon

½ teaspoon ground ginger

½ teaspoon ground green cardamom

¼ teaspoon ground nutmeg

1 teaspoon baking powder

½ teaspoon baking soda

½ teaspoon fine salt

½ cup (125 ml) vanilla-flavored almond, soy, or coconut milk

1 tablespoon cider vinegar

½ cup (100 g) organic cane sugar

⅓ cup (75 ml) canola oil

2 teaspoons vanilla extract

VEGAN CHAI BUTTERCREAM FROSTING

1 cup (221 g) vegan buttery stick, such as Earth Balance, at room temperature

6 cups (720 g) organic confectioners' sugar, sifted

1 teaspoon ground cinnamon

½ teaspoon ground ginger

½ teaspoon ground green cardamom

¼ teaspoon ground nutmeg

1 teaspoon vanilla extract

Mukhwas or other Indian candied seeds, for garnish

Preheat the oven to 350°F (180°C). Line two standard 12-cup cupcake pans with 14 paper liners and set them aside. In a small, heat-proof bowl or cup, pour the boiling water over the tea bag and let it steep until the tea is very strong, about 15 minutes. Measure out ½ cup (125 ml) of the tea for the cake and ¼ cup (60 ml) for the frosting and set each aside in separate bowls.

(recipe continues)

In a medium bowl, sift together the flour, cinnamon, ginger, cardamom, nutmeg, baking powder, baking soda, and salt. Set the bowl aside. In a separate large mixing bowl, stir together the almond milk, ½ cup (125 ml) of brewed chai tea, and vinegar. Allow the mixture to sit for 1 minute, then whisk in the cane sugar, oil, and vanilla. Whisk the flour mixture into the milk mixture, one-third at a time. Keep whisking until the batter becomes smooth and starts to thicken, about 3 minutes. Pour ¼ cup (60 ml) of the batter into each lined cupcake mold.

Bake for 16 to 18 minutes, or until a toothpick inserted in the center of a cupcake comes out clean. Remove the cupcakes from the oven and set the pans on wire racks to cool completely.

For the frosting, in the bowl of an electric mixer, beat the vegan buttery stick with the confectioners' sugar, cinnamon, ginger, cardamom, and nutmeg until well blended and very thick, about 3 minutes. Add the vanilla and the reserved ¼ cup of brewed chai tea and beat until the frosting is light and fluffy, about 2 minutes.

If you like, scoop the frosting into a piping bag fitted with a star tip and pipe the frosting onto the cooled cupcakes, or simply spread on the frosting with a knife or offset spatula. Sprinkle the cupcakes with mukhwas. If you like, scatter more mukhwas on a platter, arrange the cupcakes on it, and serve. Store the cupcakes at room temperature for up to 3 days.

"I like to stop and remember sometimes that we'll never be as young as we are right now. We only get 100 years or so to enjoy interior design, books, buffets and clean sheets, radio waves and good movie seats, bakery air, rain hair, bubble wrap and illegal naps."

Neil Pasricha, author of *The Book of Awesome: Snow Days, Bakery Air, Finding Money in Your Pocket, and Other Simple, Brilliant Things*

Rootin' Tootin' Texas Chocolate Cupcakes

I received a recipe for a chocolate sheet cake from a minister's wife, and I have tinkered with it over the years until I have it just as I like it now: smaller. These coffee-tinged chocolate cupcakes have a moist, tender texture and the perfect frosting. I made these for my daughter-in-law Jessica's baby shower and topped them with Homemade Colored Sprinkles (page 35). Instead of making cupcakes, you could make the original sheet cake in a (16½ x 11½ x 1-inch/42 x 29 x 2.5-cm) jelly-roll pan, which will take 15 to 20 minutes to bake, or until the cake pulls away from the sides of the pan.

MAKES 36 CUPCAKES

ROOTIN' TOOTIN' TEXAS CHOCOLATE CAKE

2	cups (500 g) granulated sugar
¼	teaspoon fine salt
2	cups (250 g) unbleached all-purpose flour
1	cup (227 g) unsalted butter
1	teaspoon ground cinnamon
¼	cup (30 g) unsweetened cocoa powder
1	cup (250 ml) freshly brewed dark roast coffee
2	large eggs
1	teaspoon vanilla extract
1	teaspoon baking soda
½	cup (125 ml) buttermilk

COCOA FROSTING

½	cup (113 g) unsalted butter
6	tablespoons (90 ml) whole milk
3	tablespoons unsweetened cocoa powder
1	(16-ounce/454-g) package confectioners' sugar, sifted
1	teaspoon vanilla extract

Preheat the oven to 400°F (200°C). Line three standard 12-cup cupcake pans with paper liners and set them aside.

For the Rootin' Tootin' Texas Chocolate Cake, place the sugar, salt, and flour in a large mixing bowl. In a saucepan over medium-high heat, bring the butter, cinnamon, cocoa powder, and coffee to a boil. Remove the pan from the heat and pour the cocoa mixture over the flour mixture, stirring to blend with a wooden spoon. In a small bowl, beat the eggs with a fork and add them to the batter. Stir in the vanilla, baking soda, and buttermilk and blend well. Divide the batter among the prepared cupcake liners.

Bake for 15 to 20 minutes, or until a cake tester inserted in the center of a cupcake comes out clean.

Remove the cupcakes from the oven and set them aside to cool completely in the pans.

For the Cocoa Frosting, bring the butter, milk, and cocoa powder to a boil in a medium saucepan over medium-high heat. Cook for 2 minutes, then remove the pan from the heat and whisk in the confectioners' sugar and vanilla. If necessary, transfer the frosting to a food processor to get all the lumps out. Let the frosting cool, then spread it over the cooled cupcakes and serve. Store them at room temperature for up to 3 days.

Cherry Mashers, Pollock-Style

These little yellow cakes, similar to Whoopie Pies, have a sour cherry and marshmallow filling and a final flourish of melted semisweet chocolate. Channel your inner abstract expressionist artist and make the pattern as interesting as possible, à la Jackson Pollock, whose unique painting style involved standing and dripping paint from a brush onto a canvas on the floor.

MAKES 30 SANDWICH CAKES

CHERRY MASHERS

3	cups (285 g) unbleached all-purpose flour
1	teaspoon baking soda
½	teaspoon fine salt
1	cup (227 g) unsalted butter, at room temperature
2	cups (500 g) granulated or raw sugar
3	large egg yolks
1	large egg
1½	cups (375 ml) plain Greek yogurt or sour cream
2	teaspoons vanilla extract

SOUR CHERRY AND MARSHMALLOW FILLING

6	tablespoons (90 g) unsalted butter, at room temperature
1	cup (120 g) confectioners' sugar, sifted
¼	cup (60 ml) sour cherry preserves
½	teaspoon almond extract
⅛	teaspoon fine salt
1	(7-ounce/205-g) jar marshmallow crème

CHOCOLATE GARNISH

1	cup (175 g) semisweet chocolate chips

Preheat the oven to 375°F (190°C). Line two large baking sheets with parchment paper and set them aside.

For the Cherry Mashers, sift the flour, baking soda, and salt into a medium bowl; set the bowl aside.

In the bowl of an electric mixer, cream together the butter and sugar until the mixture pale, light, and fluffy, about 3 minutes. Beat in the egg yolks and egg until well blended. Beat in the yogurt and vanilla until just blended. At low speed, beat in the flour mixture, 1 cup (250 ml) at a time, until you have a smooth batter, about 2 minutes.

Drop 1½ tablespoons of batter onto the prepared baking sheet for each cake, spacing the mounds 2½ inches (6.5 cm) apart.

Bake until the cakes are lightly golden on the edges and the tops spring back to the touch, about 8 to 10 minutes. Remove the cakes from the oven and transfer them to wire racks to cool completely.

For the Sour Cherry and Marshmallow Filling, in the bowl of a food processor or in the clean bowl of an electric mixer, process or beat together the butter, confectioners' sugar, cherry preserves, almond extract, salt, and marshmallow crème until smooth.

To assemble the Cherry Mashers, spread 1 to 2 teaspoons of filling on one little cake and top with another cake. Repeat with the remaining cakes and filling.

For the Chocolate Garnish, place the chocolate chips in small sealable plastic bag. Seal the bag and microwave on high for 12 seconds, then massage the chips in the bag to help them melt. Keep microwaving the chocolate for very short intervals and massaging until the chocolate has melted completely.

Snip a corner from the bag and squeeze decorative lines of melted chocolate across each assembled Cherry Masher. Serve right away or store the cakes in an airtight container in the refrigerator for up to 2 days.

Warm Chocolate Cakes with Lavender Whipped Cream

There's nothing better than the aroma of warm chocolate for pleasure, except, of course, the indulgence of having a small warm chocolate dessert all to yourself. Take a tip from The Inn at Cedar Falls in the Hocking Hills of Ohio, where this dessert is served: Make and freeze the unbaked cakes up to 3 days ahead, then pop them in the oven right after you've finished the main course. While you're at it, infuse lavender in the cream and refrigerate it ahead of time, too. Whip the Lavender Cream while the cakes are in the oven.

○┈┈┈┈┈┈┈┈┈┈┈┈┈┈┈ MAKES 6 SERVINGS ┈┈┈┈┈┈┈┈┈┈┈┈┈┈┈○

Unsalted butter, for the ramekins or custard cups

WARM CHOCOLATE CAKES

- ¾ cup (150 g) semisweet chocolate chips or chunks
- 10 tablespoons (150 g) unsalted butter, at room temperature
- ½ cup (100 g) granulated sugar
- 3 large eggs
- ½ cup plus 2 tablespoons (60 g) unbleached all-purpose flour
- ¼ teaspoon fine salt
- 1½ tablespoons unsweetened cocoa powder
- ¾ teaspoon baking powder

LAVENDER WHIPPED CREAM

- 1 cup Lavender Cream (page 23), chilled
- 1 tablespoon granulated sugar
  Fresh mint sprigs, for garnish

Butter the insides of six (½ cup/125 ml) ramekins or oven-safe custard cups and set them aside.

In a small saucepan over medium heat, melt the chocolate, butter, and sugar together. Transfer the mixture to the bowl of an electric mixer, add the eggs, flour, salt, cocoa, and baking powder, and beat on medium speed for about 8 minutes, or until the batter is thick and mousse-like. Divide the batter among the prepared ramekins, cover them with plastic wrap, and freeze them for at least 3 hours and up to 3 days before baking.

When you're ready to bake the cakes, preheat the oven to 375°F (190°C). Put a large, metal mixing bowl in the freezer to chill.

Take the ramekins out of the freezer, remove the plastic wrap, and place them on a baking sheet. Bake for 15 to 18 minutes or until the edges of the cakes are just set and the middles seem a little under done (these are most sumptuous if not overbaked). Remove the cakes from the oven and let them cool for 10 minutes.

For the Lavender Whipped Cream, remove the mixing bowl from the freezer. Beat the cream and sugar together in the chilled bowl with a hand-held mixer until thick and billowy, about 8 minutes.

To serve, loosen the sides of each cake by running a small knife around the perimeter, then invert each cake onto a dessert plate. Serve the cakes with a mound of Lavender Whipped Cream and a garnish fresh mint, if you like.

SO HAPPY TOGETHER

Dark Chocolate + Lavender

Surprisingly, dark chocolate goes well with lavender. These Warm Chocolate Cakes and the Miniature Chocolate Soufflés (page 77) taste a little more deep and mysterious with a lavender-infused whipped cream.

"People who need people may be the luckiest people in the world, but people who do what they like for a living are the happiest, followed closely by people who work with their hands."

Marcy Goldman, professional baker and cookbook author at
www.betterbaking.com

Razzle-Dazzle Éclairs

Éclairs were once the darlings of mom-and-pop bakeries. Based on a simple pastry that can be made in a saucepan, they were just right for small-batch baking. Now, they're making a couture comeback as the darlings of upscale bakery boutiques like Fauchon in Paris, Lafayette in New York, and Bobbette & Belle in Toronto. The traditional éclair filling would be Pastry Cream (page 22), and the traditional icing would be sweetened, melted chocolate, also delicious. Once you get started with this recipe, however, feel free to do oh-so-much more. Flavor the pastry cream (page 23). Dip the éclair into a thin icing you can flavor or color as you wish. Then sprinkle on a fun topping: Homemade Colored Sprinkles (page 35), sugar pearls, dragées, edible flower petals, or shaved chocolate. Food writer Maria Siriano of Columbus, Ohio, who blogs at Sift & Whisk, made purple-iced Blueberry-Violet Éclairs, the pastry cream and icing flavored with crème de violette liqueur. She then finished off the look with edible flowers. Stunning! These Razzle-Dazzle Éclairs are likewise pretty in pink. For a final flourish, scatter organic, unsprayed edible flower blossoms from your garden or grocery store herb section. You can form and freeze éclairs (unbaked) for up to 3 months; then thaw, bake, fill, and ice.

MAKES 2 DOZEN ÉCLAIRS

CHOUX PASTRY

½	cup (113 g) unsalted butter, cut into cubes
1	cup (250 ml) water
1	cup (125 g) unbleached all-purpose flour
1	teaspoon fine salt
4	large eggs

RASPBERRY ICING

1	cup (160 g) fresh or frozen raspberries, thawed if frozen
2	tablespoons (25 ml) granulated sugar
2	cups (240 g) confectioners' sugar, sifted
1	tablespoon whole milk
	Edible flowers, for garnish

ALMOND-FLAVORED PASTRY CREAM

Pastry Cream (page 22) flavored with 1 teaspoon almond extract

Preheat the oven to 450°F (230°C). Line a baking sheet with parchment paper. With a pencil, mark 24 (4-inch/10-cm) vertical lines spaced 2 inches (5 cm) apart on the parchment. Flip the parchment on the baking sheet (you should be able to see the lines from the clean side), and set the baking sheet aside.

For the Choux Pastry, bring the butter and water to a boil in a medium saucepan over medium-high heat. Vigorously whisk in the flour and salt all at once until the dough forms a ball in the middle of the pan. Remove the pan from the heat and scrape the dough into a food processor. Pulse in each egg, one at a time, until you have a smooth, shiny, golden dough, about 2 minutes.

To form the éclairs, fit a pastry bag with a ½-inch/1.25-cm-diameter tip. Fill the bag with the pastry, twist it closed, and squeeze the dough down until it gets to the tip. Hold your finger over the tip to keep the dough from flowing out.

(recipe continues)

Pipe the dough onto the marked lines on the parchment paper, pressing the tip of the tube at the top of a line, and gently squeezing the pastry bag while you trace down the length of each line. Start and stop the dough by pressing the tip of the tube firmly onto the parchment paper. Lift up the pastry bag to begin a new line. Refill the pastry bag as needed. When you are finished piping, you should have 24 lines of pastry dough that are about 1 inch (2.5 cm) wide and 4 inches (10 cm) long.

Bake the pastry for 15 minutes, then reduce the heat to 325°F (160°C) and bake for 10 to 15 minutes more, or until the pastry has puffed and turned shiny golden brown. Remove the éclairs from the oven and let them cool completely on the baking sheet.

For the icing, combine the raspberries and sugar in a medium saucepan over medium-high heat and cook, stirring, until the raspberries have softened, about 5 minutes. Remove the pan from the heat and strain the mixture into a medium bowl through a fine-mesh sieve lined with cheesecloth; discard the seeds. Add the confectioners' sugar and milk to the raspberry purée and whisk to combine. If necessary, add more milk until the icing just barely drips off the whisk. Set the icing aside.

To fill the éclairs, pass a wooden skewer lengthwise through the center of each éclair to make a channel. Fit a pastry bag with a plain tip, such as Wilton #230. Fill the bag with Almond-Flavored Pastry Cream.

Holding each éclair between your thumb and forefinger, pipe the pastry cream in one end until it starts to come out the other. When you feel the éclair get heavier, that is your cue to stop filling. You can also use a serrated knife to cut the éclair in half like a hot dog bun, then pipe or spoon pastry cream on the bottom half of the éclair and close.

Dip the top of each filled éclair into the icing and then place the éclairs on wire racks, icing-side up, and scatter them with the edible blossoms. The icing will cool and harden in about 30 minutes. Éclairs are best enjoyed the same day they are made.

SO HAPPY TOGETHER

Raspberry + Almond

Those two ingredients—the classic flavor duo in the Bakewell Tarts and Maids of Honour beloved by British bakers—make a classic pairing. Almond is bitter, raspberry is sharp, but with a little sugar in common, they complement each other.

Venezuelan Spiced Brownies

Adapted from a recipe by chocolatier Christopher Elbow, these brownies are especially addictive. Dense and mysterious, these are not your second grader's brownies—although he just might go for one.

1⅓ cups (303 g) unsalted butter, at room temperature, plus more for the pan

2 cups (500 g) granulated sugar

4 large eggs

2 teaspoons vanilla extract

1¼ cups (150 g) great-quality unsweetened cocoa powder, such as Valhrona

1 teaspoon ground cinnamon

½ teaspoon chipotle powder

1¾ cups (210 g) unbleached all-purpose flour, sifted

½ teaspoon fine salt

1 cup (175 g) dark chocolate chunks or semisweet chocolate chips

Preheat the oven to 350°F (180°C). Butter the inside of a 13 x 9-inch (33 x 23-cm) baking pan and set it aside.

In the bowl of an electric mixer, cream the butter and sugar together until the mixture is pale and fluffy, about 4 minutes. Beat in the eggs and vanilla until just combined. In a small bowl, combine the cocoa powder, cinnamon, and chipotle powder. In another small bowl, sift together the flour and salt. Add the cocoa mixture to the egg mixture, one-third at a time, alternating with the flour and beating well after each addition, until you have a smooth batter. Stir in the chocolate chunks with a spatula. Spoon the batter into the prepared pan and smooth the top.

Bake for 25 to 30 minutes or until the center of the brownie has set and the edges start to pull away from the pan. Remove the brownie pan from the oven and let it cool for 30 minutes, then cut into squares and serve. Store them at room temperature, covered, for up to 3 days.

SO HAPPY TOGETHER

Warm Spices + Burnt Sugar Caramel + Chocolate

Warm spices (such as cinnamon and ground chipotle) and burnt sugar caramel really accentuate the flavor of chocolate. Serve a Venezuelan Spiced Brownie in the center of a white plate. Dust the top of the brownie with confectioners' sugar. Aromatize by drizzling an artistic circle of warm Sea Salt Caramel (page 24) or Venezuelan Spiced Chocolate Ganache (page 27) around it. Top with a small scoop of ice cream.

Churros with Venezuelan Spiced Chocolate Ganache

Ay, caramba, these are good! The same choux pastry for éclairs can also make delicious baked churros. I like to serve little cups of hot chocolate ganache with these lighter and airier churros for dipping.

MAKES 2 DOZEN CHURROS

CHOUX PASTRY

½	cup (113 g) unsalted butter, cut into cubes
1	cup (250 ml) water
1	cup (125 g) unbleached all-purpose flour
1	teaspoon fine salt
4	large eggs

TOPPING

1	teaspoon ground cinnamon
¼	cup (50 g) granulated sugar
	Vegetable oil, for brushing
1	recipe Venezuelan Spiced Chocolate Ganache (page 27), prepared and warm

Preheat the oven to 450°F (230°C). Line a baking sheet with parchment paper. With a pencil, mark 24 (4-inch/10-cm) lines spaced 2 inches (5 cm) apart. Flip the parchment on the baking sheet (you should be able to see the lines from the clean side), and set the baking sheet aside.

For the Choux Pastry, bring the butter and water to a boil in a medium saucepan over medium-high heat. Vigorously whisk in the flour and salt all at once until the dough forms a ball in the middle of the pan. Remove the pan from the heat and scrape the dough into a food processor. Pulse in each egg, one at a time, until you have a smooth, shiny, golden dough, about 2 minutes.

Fit the end of a pastry bag with a star tip, such as #867 or French Star #7. Fill the bag with the dough, twist it closed, and squeeze the dough down until it gets to the tip. Hold your finger over the tip to keep the dough from flowing out.

Pipe the dough onto the marked lines on the parchment paper, pressing the tip of the tube at the top of a line, and gently squeezing the pastry bag while you trace down the length of each line. Start and stop the dough by pressing the tip of the tube firmly onto the parchment paper. Lift up the pastry bag to begin a new line. Refill the pastry bag as needed. When you are finished piping, you should have 24 lines of pastry dough that are about 1 inch (2.5 cm) wide and 4 inches (10 cm) long. For the topping, mix the cinnamon and sugar together in a small bowl. Gently brush the churros with vegetable oil and sprinkle them with the cinnamon sugar.

Bake for 15 minutes, then reduce the heat to 325°F (160°C) and bake for 10 to 15 minutes more, or until the churros have puffed and turned shiny golden brown. Remove the churros from the oven and let them cool on the baking sheet. To serve, dip the churros in the warm chocolate ganache. These are best enjoyed the same day they are made.

Chapter Seven

CUSTARDS, FLANS, and BREAD PUDDINGS

VOLUPTUOUS CUSTARD DISHES—FROM BAKED CUSTARDS to flans and bread puddings—are all about smooth texture. These desserts center around eggs and especially egg yolks to provide body and golden color. To get a lump-free custard, strain the mixture through a fine-mesh sieve and then bake it in a water bath or bain-marie—a large pan with enough water to come up the sides of the baking dish or custard cups you put in it to bake.

A custard is a classic blank canvas that you can paint with color and flavor. Add flavor by steeping herbs, citrus, spices, or other fruits in the milk or cream to be added to the eggs, as in Fennel, Lavender, and Lemon-Scented Custard (page 181) or Saffron Crème Brûlée with Rosy Strawberry Compote (page 183). You can also bake fruits into the custard, as in Rum and Pineapple Flan (page 189) or Persimmon Flans with Honeyed Whipped Cream (page 187).

To finish off a custard dish, you can always add a frill of piped Loop-de-Loop Italian Meringue (page 67) or Swiss Meringue (page 66), and use up the rest of the egg whites at the same time. Sprinkle the meringue with Homemade Colored Sprinkles (page 35), an aromatic gremolata similar to Sweet Orange Mint Gremolata (page 90), or cookie dust.

Fennel, Lavender, and Lemon–Scented Custard

If you've only tasted plain English-style custard, you'll love the vivid character of this one flavored with fennel seed, dried lavender buds, and fresh lemon. I've also added vanilla for smoothness. The mixture of eggs and egg yolks give this custard a voluptuous texture. Use the leftover egg whites to make meringues (see Chapter Three, page 63) or Swiss Meringue Buttercream Frosting (page 205).

MAKES 6 SERVINGS

1   teaspoon fennel seed
1   teaspoon dried culinary-grade lavender buds
1   (2 x ½-inch/5 x 1.25-cm) strip fresh lemon peel
2   cups (500 ml) whole milk
3   large eggs
5   large egg yolks
½   cup (125 ml) heavy whipping cream
⅓   cup (67 g) granulated sugar
⅛   teaspoon fine salt
1   teaspoon vanilla extract
    Fresh lavender sprigs and lemon peel, for garnish

Preheat the oven to 350°F (180°C).

With a mortar and pestle or in a clean coffee or spice grinder, coarsely crush or grind the fennel seed to a fine powder. Transfer the crushed fennel seed to a medium saucepan, along with the lavender, lemon peel, and milk, and bring the mixture to a boil over medium-high heat. Remove the pan from the heat, cover it, and let the mixture steep for 15 minutes. Strain the milk through a fine-mesh sieve lined with cheesecloth into a medium bowl, then strain it again back into the saucepan; discard the solids.

In a medium bowl, whisk together the eggs and egg yolks, then add them to the saucepan, and whisk them into the milk along with the the cream, sugar, salt, and vanilla. Strain the custard mixture into another bowl, then ladle the custard into six individual custard cups or small baking dishes.

Set the filled cups in a deep baking dish, and fill the baking dish with enough hot water to reach halfway up the sides of the custard cups.

Bake the custards for 20 to 30 minutes, or until a knife inserted near the edge of a custard cup comes out clean. Remove the pan from the oven and set the custards on a kitchen towel to cool. When the custards have cooled to room temperature, cover them with plastic wrap and chill them in the refrigerator for 1 hour before serving.

Saffron Crème Brûlée with Rosy Strawberry Compote

I have a late-eighteenth- or early-nineteenth-century glazed chintz quilt from Pennsylvania in gorgeous earthy colors of pale gold, warm brown, and rose red, the colors of the dessert. Saffron, one of the most precious flavorings in the world, is made from the dried pistils of a certain type of crocus and is available at better grocery stores, at Asian or Middle Eastern markets, and online. A spoonful of brûlée together with a rosy-flavored strawberry is simply wonderful, and brings to mind my quilt. Adapted from a recipe by pastry-chef-turned-artisan-chocolate-maker Christopher Elbow, both the crème brûlée and the compote can be made a day ahead. When strawberries are not in season, serve this crème brûlée with a scattering of pomegranate seeds and a drizzle of grenadine mixed with a drop or two of rosewater. With all the egg whites left over, it will be a great time to head to the Meringue Chapter (page 63).

MAKES 8 TO 10 (6-OUNCE/175-ML) RAMEKINS

SAFFRON CRÈME BRÛLÉE

1   quart (1 L) heavy whipping cream
1   cup (200 g) granulated sugar, divided
¼   teaspoon saffron threads
10 large egg yolks

ROSY STRAWBERRY COMPOTE

2   pints (576 g) fresh strawberries, hulled
¼   cup (60 ml) grenadine
    Zest of 1 orange
    Zest of 1 lemon
2   tablespoons rosewater

TOPPING

8   to 10 tablespoons (110 to 125 g) packed light brown sugar

For the Saffron Crème Brûlée, preheat the oven to 375°F (190°C). Whisk the cream, ½ cup (100 g) of the sugar, and the saffron together in a heavy-bottomed saucepan over medium heat. Scald the cream until small bubbles form around the perimeter of the pan. Do not let the cream boil. Remove the pan from the heat, cover it, and let the cream infuse for 5 minutes.

Meanwhile, in the bowl of an electric mixer, beat the egg yolks with the remaining ½ cup (100 g) of sugar until the mixture turns a pale yellow, about 3 minutes. Slowly beat in the hot cream, then pass the batter through a fine-mesh sieve back into the saucepan. Divide the mixture among eight to ten (6-ounce/175-ml) ramekins or small ovenproof bowls. Set the ramekins in a baking pan and fill the pan with enough hot water to reach halfway up the sides of the ramekins. Cover the baking pan with aluminum foil and place it in the oven. Immediately reduce the oven temperature to 325°F (160°C).

(recipe continues)

Bake for 30 minutes, or until the crème brûlées are just set but the centers still move a bit when gently shaken. Remove the pan from the oven and set the ramekins on a kitchen towel to cool, about 30 minutes. Cover the ramekins with plastic wrap and refrigerate them for at least 4 hours or overnight.

For the Rosy Strawberry Compote, in a large bowl, toss together the strawberries, grenadine, orange zest, lemon zest, and rosewater. Cover the bowl and refrigerate the compote for at least 4 hours or overnight.

To serve, preheat the broiler. Place the ramekins in a baking pan with enough cool water to reach halfway up the sides of each ramekin. Sprinkle a tablespoon of brown sugar on top of each ramekin and broil until the sugar bubbles and melts. Immediately remove the ramekins from the oven and serve the crème brûlée with the compote. Cover and refrigerate any leftover crème brûlées for up to 1 day; the hard sugar shell will soften, so consider waiting to melt the sugar on any that may be left over.

"The saffron stained my tiny fingers crimson and left a lingering aroma: the smell of happiness."

Monica Bhide, food writer and cookbook author

Fresh Pumpkin Flan

Somewhere between a flan and a cheesecake in texture, this moist and delicious burnt orange–colored flan has a thin coating of caramel when it is turned out of the pan. Use small sugar or pie pumpkins that arrive at the market in October, or in a pinch, use unsweetened canned pumpkin. This is gorgeous garnished with red, yellow, orange, or variegated nasturtium flowers and leaves.

MAKES 8 SERVINGS

1½ pounds (750 g) fresh pumpkin, peeled, seeded, and cut into pieces

1 quart (1 L) water

2 cups (400 g) granulated sugar, divided

2 tablespoons unsalted butter

½ cup (60 g) unbleached all-purpose flour

2 cups (500 ml) whole milk

1 teaspoon fine salt

½ teaspoon vanilla extract

4 large eggs
Edible flowers for garnish

Place the pumpkin and water in a large saucepan over high heat and bring the water to a boil. Reduce the heat to medium-low, cover the pan, and simmer until the pumpkin is tender, about 30 minutes.

Place a wire rack on a flat work surface. Pour 1 cup (200 g) of the sugar in the bottom of an 8-inch (20-cm) round metal cake pan. Place the pan directly on a burner over medium heat. When the sugar has melted and turned a light golden color, after about 10 minutes, put an oven mitt on one hand and carefully swirl the pan to coat the bottom and sides with the caramel. Remove the pan from the heat and place it on the wire rack.

Preheat the oven to 350°F (180°C).

Drain the pumpkin and place it in the bowl of an electric mixer. Add the butter to the bowl and beat until the mixture is smooth. Beat in the flour and milk a little at a time, alternating between the two, then beat in the salt, vanilla, and the remaining 1 cup (203 g) of sugar until you have a smooth batter. Beat in the eggs, one at a time. Pour the batter through a fine-mesh sieve into the caramelized cake pan and place the pan in a large, shallow baking pan filled with 1 inch (2.5 cm) of hot water.

Bake for 2 hours, or until the flan has pulled away from the sides of the pan and a cake tester inserted in the center comes out clean. Remove the pan from the oven, and transfer the flan to a wire rack to cool.

When the flan has cooled for about 1 hour, invert it onto a rimmed cakestand or serving plate. Garnish the flan with fresh flowers and serve. Cover and store them at room temperature for up to 2 days.

Persimmon Flans with Honeyed Whipped Cream

This dessert marries regional ingredients like native persimmons and wildflower honey with traditional Mexican flan and French crème caramel. As an alternative to the heavier pumpkin pie, persimmon flans can be a welcome addition to your cold weather or holiday menu repertoire. Even better for holiday entertaining, the flans can be made the night before and actually improve in flavor overnight. Cinnamon, coriander, and nutmeg add aromatic interest to the sweet and mellow persimmon; wildflower honey completes the trio of flavors.

MAKES 8 SERVINGS

2½ cups (500 g) granulated sugar, divided

1 teaspoon ground cinnamon

1 teaspoon ground coriander

¼ teaspoon freshly ground nutmeg

6 large eggs

1 cup (250 ml) native persimmon pulp or the pulp from 3 to 4 ripe Asian persimmons

1 (12-ounce/375-g) can unsweetened evaporated (not sweetened condensed) milk

1 teaspoon vanilla extract

   Juice of 1 large lemon

½ cup (125 ml) water

1 cup (250 ml) heavy whipping cream

½ cup (170 g) wildflower, tupelo, clover, or other amber honey

Preheat the oven to 350°F (180°C). Assemble eight (6 to 8-ounce/175 to 250-ml) custard cups or ramekins on a flat work surface.

In the bowl of an electric mixer, combine 1 cup (200 g) of the sugar with the cinnamon, coriander, and nutmeg. Beating constantly on moderate speed, add the eggs to the bowl, one at a time. Add the persimmon pulp and beat just until the batter comes together. Add the evaporated milk, vanilla, and lemon juice and beat once more until the batter is smooth. Set the bowl aside.

In a heavy-bottomed saucepan, combine the remaining 1½ cups (300 g) of sugar with the water and cook over medium heat, without stirring, until the mixture caramelizes and turns dark amber, about 15 to 20 minutes. When the sugar has caramelized, immediately remove the pan from the heat. Wearing an oven mitt on the hand that holds the saucepan, carefully pour a little caramel into the bottom of each custard cup.

(recipe continues)

Spoon about ⅓ cup (75 ml) of the persimmon batter on top of the caramel in each cup. Set the filled custard cups in a deep-sided baking dish and pour enough water into the pan to reach halfway up the sides of the cups. Cover the baking dish with foil.

Bake for 35 to 40 minutes, or until the flans are set and a cake tester inserted in the center of a flan comes out clean. Remove the baking dish from the oven and transfer the custard cups to a kitchen towel to cool. Cover each flan with plastic wrap and refrigerate them for at least 1 hour or up to 2 days, until ready to serve.

When you're ready to serve the flans, in the clean bowl of an electric mixer, whip the cream until soft peaks form. Blend in the honey, and whip again until stiffer peaks form. Remove the flans from the refrigerator and run a small paring knife around the rim of each. Hold a dessert plate over the top of each flan and invert it so that the flan and the caramel are positioned in the center of the plate. Place a dollop of honeyed whipped cream on each portion and serve. Cover and refrigerate any leftover flans for up to 2 days.

Rum and Pineapple Flan

From the Spanish culinary influence in the Caribbean and the American Southwest, we get dessert recipes like flan. Most flans have a very smooth, velvety texture. This one does, too, but it also has caramelized bits of baked pineapple as a wonderful foil. Serve this drizzled with a little heavy whipping cream if you want to gild the lily.

MAKES 1 (10-INCH/25-CM) FLAN

2	cups (330 g) fresh pineapple cut into 1-inch chunks
1½	cups (375 ml) whole milk
1	vanilla bean, split lengthwise
½	cup (125 ml) rum
3	large eggs
3	large egg yolks
⅔	cup (130 g) granulated sugar
2	tablespoons unbleached all-purpose flour
2	tablespoons heavy whipping cream

Preheat the oven to 400°F (200°C).

Butter a shallow, 10-inch (25-cm) round baking or soufflé dish and scatter the pineapple chunks on the bottom. Bake the pineapple for 20 minutes or until it has slightly caramelized. Remove the dish from the oven and set it aside to cool slightly.

Reduce the oven temperature to 350°F (180°C).

Pour the milk into a heavy saucepan over medium heat. Scrape the vanilla seeds into the milk, then drop in the vanilla bean pod. Bring the mixture to a simmer and cook for 2 minutes or until small bubbles form around the perimeter of the pan. Remove the pan from the heat, cover it, and let the milk steep for 15 minutes. Remove the vanilla bean and whisk in the rum.

In a medium bowl, whisk together the eggs, egg yolks, sugar, flour, and cream until smooth. Gradually whisk in the hot milk mixture. Pour the custard over the pineapple in the baking dish.

Bake for 30 minutes, or until a knife inserted in the center of the flan comes out clean.

Remove the flan from the oven and let it cool slightly, then spoon it into individual bowls and serve it warm or at room temperature.

Aromatic Rice Pudding

The first time I had rice pudding flavored with fresh bay leaf was during an Indian cooking class when I lived in London. Bay leaf has a fresh yet haunting flavor, like a film that stays with you long after it is over. It's worth seeking out fresh California bay leaves—or buying a small plant that you can keep in a sunny window. By the time a bay leaf has dried and faded in a spice jar, it is a ghost of its fresh self. Kaffir lime leaves, which have a citrus flavor popular in Thai food, will also work in this recipe.

MAKES 8 SERVINGS

Unsalted butter, at room temperature, for the dish
1½ cups (375 ml) whole or 2% milk
1 bay leaf, preferably fresh
1¼ cups (262 g) long grain rice
½ teaspoon fine salt
½ cup (100 g) granulated sugar
2 large eggs, separated
1 teaspoon vanilla extract
2 tablespoons melted unsalted butter
1 teaspoon freshly grated lemon zest
Shelled, unsalted pistachios, coarsely chopped, for garnish
Edible flower petals, for garnish

Preheat the oven to 350°F (180°C). Butter a 2-quart (2-L) round baking dish and set it aside.

Combine the milk and bay leaf in a saucepan over medium heat. Bring the milk to a simmer, then cover the pan, remove it from the heat, and let the milk infuse for 30 minutes. Remove and discard the bay leaf.

In a medium saucepan, cook the rice according to package directions, about 15 minutes. Rinse the hot rice with cold water to remove the starch, then drain it well. Place the rice in a large mixing bowl. Blot the rice with a paper towel to remove extra moisture, if necessary. In a separate, medium bowl, whisk together the salt, sugar, egg yolks, infused milk, vanilla, melted butter, and lemon zest. Pour this mixture over the rice and mix well with a spatula or wooden spoon.

In another bowl, whip the egg whites until they are stiff and fold them into the rice mixture. Spoon the rice into the prepared baking dish and bake for 1 hour, or until the pudding is golden brown and a cake tester inserted in the center comes out clean.

Remove the dish from the oven and let the pudding cool slightly before serving, garnished with pistachios and edible flower petals. Cover and chill any leftovers in the refrigerator for up to 2 days.

Bay Leaf + Cream

For the late British food writer and cookbook author Elizabeth David, who re-introduced good cooking to Britain after the stodgy food of World War II, "a freshly picked bay leaf gives out a strange scent, bitter and aromatic, with something of both vanilla and nutmeg and can be boiled in milk for a bechamel sauce or a sweet cream with good results." The dominant flavor compound in fresh bay, called cineole—also found in rosemary and cardamom—produces a cooling, lingering taste.

"Always serve too much hot fudge sauce.... It makes people overjoyed, and puts them in your debt."

Judith Olney, author of *The Joy of Chocolate*

Sweet Potato Pone with Bourbon Pouring Custard

Also known as pain patate, *this baked pudding has Creole roots and used to be sold by street vendors in New Orleans. Today, it's a Jazz Fest must-have, along with crawfish gumbo and spinach and artichoke casserole. Somehow, "crème anglaise" seems too fancy a term for the pouring custard accompanying this dessert, but that's what it is. This classic French accompaniment, dressed-down, is also good over sautéed apples, spiced pound cake, a warm chocolate brownie, or baked pears.*

MAKES 6 TO 8 SERVINGS

BOURBON POURING CUSTARD

1	cup (250 ml) heavy whipping cream
3	large egg yolks
¼	cup (50 g) granulated sugar
⅛	teaspoon fine salt
¼	cup (60 ml) bourbon

SWEET POTATO PONE

3	cups (350 g) peeled and grated raw sweet potatoes, from about 2 large
½	cup (100 g) granulated sugar
¼	cup (30 g) unbleached all-purpose flour
2	large eggs
½	cup (125 ml) pure cane syrup, dark molasses, or sorghum
1	teaspoon freshly grated nutmeg
1	teaspoon ground cinnamon
1	teaspoon vanilla extract
4	tablespoons (60 g) unsalted butter, melted, plus more for the skillet

For the Bourbon Pouring Custard, scald the cream in a heavy saucepan over medium-high heat until small bubbles start to form around the perimeter, about 4 minutes.

In a medium bowl, whisk together the egg yolks, sugar, and salt. Pour a little of the hot cream into the egg yolk mixture, whisking constantly. Transfer the egg yolk and cream mixture back to the saucepan and cook over low heat until the mixture has thickened and coats the back of a spoon, about 10 to 15 minutes. Stir in the bourbon. Pass the custard through a fine-mesh sieve into a large bowl to remove any lumps. Cover the bowl and refrigerate the custard until ready to serve. Let it come to room temperature before serving. (The pouring custard can be made and refrigerated up to 3 days in advance.)

Preheat the oven to 350°F (180°C). Generously butter the inside of a 10-inch (25-cm) cast iron skillet or round casserole dish, and set it aside.

For the Sweet Potato Pone, in a large bowl, mix together the sweet potatoes, sugar, flour, eggs, cane syrup, nutmeg, cinnamon, and vanilla. Pour the melted butter into the bowl and mix well. Spoon the sweet potato mixture into the prepared skillet or dish and smooth the top.

Bake for 50 minutes, or until a toothpick inserted in the center of the pone comes out clean.

Remove the skillet or dish from the oven and let it cool slightly before serving. To serve, slice or scoop the pone onto individual plates and serve it with Bourbon Pouring Custard. Cover and chill any leftovers in the refrigerator for up to 2 days.

French Chocolate Bread Puddings

Adapted from a recipe by Life's a Feast blogger Jamie Schler, who lives in France, this bread pudding is sumptuously simple. Instead of pieces of bread soaked in custard, this method involves grinding stale brioche, challah, or cookies to a fine powder before soaking, so the resulting texture is velvety smooth. Again, this is a recipe you can customize to suit your taste. Use chocolate wafer cookies, gingersnaps, cinnamon Biscoff cookies, or any other flavored thin and crispy cookie. Adjust the added spice to suit the bread or cookie. Aromatize these little puddings before serving with warmed Spice Syrup (page 28) or Sea Salt Caramel (page 24).

○ · MAKES 10 INDIVIDUAL BREAD PUDDINGS · ○

Unsalted butter, for the ramekins

2⅔ cups (600 ml) whole milk

½ cup (100 g) granulated sugar

7 ounces (198 g) dark, 70% cacao semisweet or bittersweet chocolate, finely chopped

1¼ cups (150 g) chocolate wafer, gingersnap, or Biscoff cookie crumbs, or a combination

3 large eggs

½ teaspoon ground cinnamon (optional)

½ teaspoon vanilla extract

Preheat the oven to 375°F (190°C). Lightly butter ten (4-ounce/125-ml) ramekins and set them aside.

Combine the milk and sugar in a large saucepan over medium-low heat. Bring the mixture to a boil, then immediately remove the pan from the heat. Add the chocolate to the hot milk mixture and let it rest for 3 minutes, then whisk until the chocolate has melted and turned glossy. Stir in the cookie crumbs; set the pan aside.

In a small bowl, whisk together the eggs with the cinnamon and vanilla. Pour ½ cup (125 ml) of the hot chocolate mixture into the eggs, whisking to blend. Pour the eggs into the saucepan in a slow, steady stream while whisking constantly. Divide the hot mixture among the prepared ramekins. Set the ramekins in a deep-sided baking dish and pour enough hot water around them to reach halfway up the sides of the cups.

Bake for 25 to 30 minutes or until the puddings have set. Remove the baking dish from the oven and very carefully transfer each bread pudding from the water bath to a kitchen towel to cool, about 30 minutes. Serve right from the ramekin or be brave and loosen the sides with a table knife and invert onto serving plates. Cover and chill leftover bread puddings for up to 3 days. They're delicious for breakfast.

Montmorency Bread Pudding

In June, when tart, red Montmorency cherries ripen, home cooks get busy picking, pitting, and then freezing or turning these fruits into wonderful summertime desserts. At my local farmers' market, I can buy quarts of locally grown, already pitted (what a luxury!) frozen Montmorency cherries. But if you pit the cherries yourself, a clean hair pin or even a large paper clip works well: poke straight through the cherry, pushing the pit out the other side. The idea is to remove the pit, while preserving the shape of the cherry.

MAKES 1 (13 X 9-INCH/33 X 23-CM) BREAD PUDDING

3   large eggs

¼   cup (50 g) granulated sugar

1   teaspoon vanilla extract

½   cup (100 g) mascarpone cheese, at room temperature

2   cups (500 ml) whole milk

4   tablespoons (60 g) unsalted butter, melted, plus more for buttering the pan

⅛   teaspoon freshly grated nutmeg

½   teaspoon ground cinnamon

1   cup (150 g) fresh, frozen and thawed, or canned and drained tart red cherries, pitted

½   cup (125 ml) sour cherry preserves

12   slices brioche, challah, or other good-quality bread, crusts trimmed

Preheat the oven to 350°F (180°C). Butter a 13 x 9-inch (33 x 23-cm) baking dish and set it aside.

In a large mixing bowl, whisk together the eggs, sugar, vanilla, mascarpone cheese, milk, melted butter, nutmeg, and cinnamon until smooth. Stir in the cherries, and set the bowl aside.

Generously spread the cherry preserves on the top side only of each slice of bread. Place six of the prepared bread slices in the bottom of the baking dish, overlapping if necessary. Pour in enough of the batter to just cover the surface of the bread slices, making sure that the cherries are equally distributed. Add the remaining six prepared bread slices, and pour over the remaining cherry batter. Set the baking dish aside to soak for 20 minutes before baking. (The bread pudding can be made up to this point a few hours or the night before serving, covered, and refrigerated.)

Set the prepared pan in a deep-sided baking dish and pour enough hot water around it to reach halfway up the sides of the pan.

Bake for 50 to 60 minutes, or until a knife inserted in the center of the pudding comes out clean.

Remove the pudding from the oven and let it cool slightly before cutting and serving. Cover and chill any leftovers in the refrigerator for up to 2 days.

Blood Orange Curd Bread Pudding

The first surprise in this comforting bread pudding is the tang of Blood Orange Curd (page 19), which you can make from scratch in minutes. The second is the colorful look of it, which couldn't be easier to accomplish. Simply shingle the curd-slathered slices of brioche or pound cake upright in a loaf pan, then pour the custard over all, scatter with berries, and bake.

MAKES 6 SERVINGS

6   to 10 slices brioche or pound cake, homemade (page 217), or storebought (they should fill your loaf pan, sitting at a slight angle rather than fully upright)

4   tablespoons (60 g) unsalted butter, at room temperature, plus more for the pan

1   recipe Blood Orange Curd (page 19), prepared

⅓   cup (67 g) granulated sugar

2   large eggs

1   large egg yolk

1¼ cups whole milk or half-and-half

1   cup (150 g) fresh blueberries or blackberries

Butter a 9 x 5-inch (23 x 13-cm) loaf pan and set it aside.

Spread each bread or pound cake slice with about ½ tablespoon of the butter, then spread each slice liberally with curd on the top side only. Place the prepared bread slices upright, shingled, in the prepared pan.

In a large mixing bowl, whisk together the sugar, eggs, and milk, and pour the mixture over the bread in the loaf pan.

Let the mixture stand for at least 30 minutes to saturate the bread. (The bread pudding can be made up to this point a few hours or the night before serving, covered, and refrigerated.)

When you're ready to bake the pudding, preheat the oven to 325°F (160°C).

Set the prepared pan in a deep-sided baking dish and pour enough hot water around it to reach halfway up the sides of the pan. Scatter the berries on top of the soaked bread. Bake for 45 to 55 minutes or until a knife inserted in the center of the pudding comes out clean.

Remove the pudding from the oven and let it cool slightly before cutting and serving.

VARIATIONS

IF YOU LIKE, VARY THE CURD AND THE BERRIES—try Meyer Lemon Curd (page 20) with pomegranate seeds, Lemon Curd (page 20) with raspberries, Lime Curd (page 20) with blackberries, or Passion Fruit and Orange Curd (page 20) with blueberries.

Coffee Bread and Butter Pudding

How could anyone resist this pudding of brandy-soaked raisins, buttery brioche, and coffee-flavored custard? I know I can't. Besides being irresistible, this dessert is also great for entertaining—as you can make it ahead of time—and your guests will go home happy. Enjoy leftover pudding as an indulgent breakfast the morning after, and use the leftover egg whites to make meringues (see Chapter Three, page 63).

············ MAKES 1 (13 X 9-INCH/33 X 23-CM) PUDDING ············

⅔ cup (90 g) golden or dark raisins

½ cup (125 ml) brandy or cognac

6 cups (1.5 L) half-and-half or light cream

¾ cup (175 ml) finely ground French roast or espresso coffee

½ cup (113 g) unsalted butter, at room temperature, plus more for the pan

12 slices brioche, challah, or other good-quality bread, crusts trimmed

½ cup (100 g) granulated sugar

4 large eggs

6 large egg yolks

   Confectioners's sugar, for dusting

Several hours or the night before baking, combine the raisins and the brandy in a small bowl, and set it aside to soak until the raisins are plump.

Butter the inside of a 13 x 9-inch (33 x 23-cm) baking dish and set it aside.

In a large saucepan over medium-high heat, combine the half-and-half and ground coffee. Slowly bring the mixture to the boil, then remove the pan from the heat, cover it, and let the mixture infuse for 30 minutes.

Butter the bread slices on both sides and place six of them, overlapping if necessary, in the bottom of the prepared pan. Sprinkle the bread with the brandied raisins and half of the sugar. Top with the remaining six buttered bread slices and sprinkle with the remaining sugar. Set the dish aside.

In a medium bowl, whisk together the eggs and egg yolks. Strain the infused coffee cream through a fine-mesh sieve into the egg mixture and whisk until well blended. Pour the egg and cream mixture through the sieve over the buttered brioche in the pan. Set the pan aside to soak for at least 30 minutes before baking. (The bread pudding can be made up to this point a few hours or the night before serving, covered, and refrigerated.)

When you're ready to bake the pudding, preheat the oven to 350°F (180°C). Set the pan in a deep-sided baking dish and pour enough hot water around it to reach halfway up the sides of the pan.

Bake for 30 to 40 minutes, or until the pudding is browned and bubbling and a knife inserted in the center comes out clean.

Remove the pudding from the oven and let it cool slightly before serving. Serve the pudding warm or cold, dusted with confectioners' sugar.

Peanut Butter Bread Pudding with Hot Fudge Sauce

I love not-too-sweet chocolate-covered peanut butter candy. That same flavor comes through in this dessert. Originally made from peanuts grown in the South, peanut butter first debuted as a health food at the 1904 World's Fair in St. Louis. Soon, however, adults and children both discovered that a peanut butter sandwich was hard to beat, healthy or not. Roasted almond butter also works well for this dessert.

MAKES 1 (13 X 9-INCH/33 X 23-CM) BREAD PUDDING

Baking spray

1   cup (275 g) crunchy peanut butter or roasted almond butter

12 slices brioche, challah, or other good-quality bread, crusts trimmed

4   cups (1 L) half-and-half

3   large eggs

2   large egg yolks

¾   cup (160 g) granulated sugar

1   tablespoon vanilla extract

¼   teaspoon fine salt

Hot Fudge Sauce (page 25) or good-quality bottled hot fudge sauce, prepared and warmed

Spray a 13 x 9-inch (33 x 23-cm) baking pan with baking spray and set it aside.

Spread the peanut butter on the top side only of each bread slice. Arrange the slices in the baking pan in a single layer, peanut butter–side up.

In a large bowl, whisk together the half-and-half, eggs, and egg yolks. Whisk in the sugar, vanilla, and salt. Pour this mixture over the bread in the pan. Cover the pan and refrigerate it for at least an hour or overnight.

Preheat the oven to 350°F (180°C). Set the prepared pan in a deep-sided baking dish and pour enough hot water around it to reach halfway up the sides of the pan.

Bake for 45 to 55 minutes, or until a knife inserted into the center of the bread pudding comes out clean. Remove the pudding from the oven and let it cool in the pan for 30 minutes before serving.

To serve, cut individual portions of the bread pudding and top with a drizzle of hot fudge sauce.

Cover and chill any leftovers in the refrigerator for up to 2 days.

Chapter Eight

CAKES

CAKE SENDS A SIGNAL THAT THE OCCASION IS SPECIAL, that you're celebrating a milestone in someone's life. Maybe that milestone is simply the first time you've gotten together with friends in a while. Or maybe it's a "big birthday" of a family member or a last goodbye. Cake is special, so it should look and taste special, too.

Start out by making absolutely sure you can get your cake out of the pan. There's nothing worse than planning a special cake and baking it, only to have it stick. I like to use pre-cut parchment paper rounds to fit 8- or 9-inch (20- or 23-cm) pans, available online through King Arthur Flour or at cake decorating shops. Unless the recipe calls for traditional butter and a dusting of flour in the pan, I use baking spray, then the parchment paper round, and then I spray it again.

Creaming the butter and sugar together adds lightness to a cake. Keep beating the mixture until it is almost white, the signal that you've beaten enough air into it. This step can take from 5 to 7 minutes. Don't rush it.

For the tenderest crumb, use cake flour. Once you add the flour to the cake batter, mix it gently as you don't want the same muscular structure in your cake as you have in kneaded bread.

Add the final flourish to a layer cake like Rainbow Cake with Robin's Egg Blue Frosting (page 218) or Strawberry Birthday Cake (page 221) with a cake banner that you can find on Etsy. Or aromatize a single-layer cake such as Cane Syrup Ginger-bread (page 208) with warmed Vanilla Baked Apricots (page 58); Almond Keeping Cake (page 211) with warm Chocolate Ganache (page 27) or Hot Fudge Sauce (page 25); or Crackly-Top Pear Cake with Warm Pear Caramel (page 207).

Celebrate and indulge!

"Anyone who spends any time in the kitchen eventually comes to realize that what he or she is looking for is the perfect chocolate cake."

Laurie Colwin, novelist and cookbook author

Flavored Syrup Buttercream Frosting

It's great to have flavoring and sweetening all in one to create a signature cake frosting. A take on the traditional American buttercream made with butter, confectioners' sugar, and a liquid, this tastes fabulous made with Rosy Strawberry Syrup (page 29) on Strawberry Birthday Cake (page 221).

MAKES ABOUT 5 CUPS (1.25 L), ENOUGH FOR ONE 3-LAYER CAKE

2   cups (454 g) unsalted butter, at room temperature
1   teaspoon vanilla extract
1   cup (250 ml) Rosy Strawberry Syrup (page 29), Passion Fruit Syrup (page 31), or bottled red raspberry or blueberry syrup
7½   cups (940 g) confectioners' sugar, sifted

In the bowl of an electric mixer, beat the butter until it is light and fluffy, about 5 minutes. Add the vanilla and syrup, beat well to combine, and then beat in the confectioners' sugar, 1 cup (120 g) at a time, until the frosting is thick, fluffy, and well blended.

Use the frosting right away or cover the bowl and refrigerate it for up to 3 days. Let the frosting come to room temperature before using.

Swiss Meringue Buttercream Frosting

You can never have too much of this silky-textured, light-and-airy frosting for layer cakes, cupcakes, or cookies. You'll need to follow the steps carefully, as this recipe, a favorite of wedding cake bakers, needs your full attention. When you're adding the butter, the frosting may look like it's separating, but just have faith—keep beating until it all comes together at the end. Although you can make this with a hand-held mixer, a sturdy stand mixer certainly proves its worth. With a stand mixer, use the whisk attachment for whipping the egg whites and then switch to the paddle attachment to beat in the butter.

MAKES ABOUT 5 CUPS (1.25 L), ENOUGH FOR ONE 3-LAYER CAKE

5	large egg whites
1	cup plus 2 tablespoons (224 g) granulated sugar
¼	teaspoon fine salt
2	cups (454 g) unsalted butter, cut into tablespoons, at room temperature
1½	teaspoons vanilla extract
	Gel food coloring, if desired

In a small saucepan or in the bottom of a double boiler, bring about 2 inches of water to a simmer over medium heat. Place a medium metal mixing bowl or the top of the double boiler over the water, but do not let the water touch the bottom of the bowl. Add the egg whites, sugar, and salt to the bowl or top of the double boiler. Whisk the mixture by hand, constantly, until an instant-read thermometer inserted in the mixture registers 160°F (75°C) and you can rub the warm mixture between your fingers and feel no sugar grit, about 5 minutes.

Remove the pan from the heat and transfer the egg mixture to the bowl of an electric mixer fitted with the whisk attachment. Beat the mixture on medium-low speed for several minutes until the sugared egg whites become foamy. Increase the speed to medium-high and beat for several minutes until the egg whites are white and soft peaks form, then increase the speed to high and whip the egg whites until they are white and glossy, and stiff peaks form that just fall over at the tip when you test with your finger. Beating the egg whites should take a total of about 10 minutes.

(recipe continues)

Once the eggs whites have formed stiff peaks, switch to the paddle attachment on the electric mixer and begin to add the butter, a tablespoon at a time, beating on medium speed and mixing well after each addition. When all the butter has been incorporated, beat in the vanilla, food coloring, or any other desired flavorings until the buttercream is smooth and thick.

Use the frosting right away or store it, covered, in the refrigerator for up to 1 week. Let the frosting come to room temperature before using.

SO HAPPY TOGETHER

Pear + Lemon

Ripe pears have a soft, romantic side—probably because they're essentially French. Think of all the wonderful pear varieties—Anjou, Comice, Bosc, Concorde, Williams' Bon Chrétien (known as Bartlett in North America)—and you conjure up a buttery, juicy fruit with an almost floral perfume. Lemon helps nudge pear along, not letting it get too dreamy.

Crackly-Top Pear Cake with Warm Pear Caramel

For an autumn dessert, this simple cake is a standout. The lemon helps give an outline to pear's impressionistic nature. And the Warm Pear Caramel rounds it out at the end. Perfect.

○ ·········· MAKES 1 (10-INCH/25-CM) CAKE ·········· ○

CRACKLY-TOP PEAR CAKE

1	tablespoon unsalted butter, plus more for the pan
5	to 6 ripe but firm pears, such as Kieffer or Bartlett, peeled, cored, and thinly sliced
⅔	cup (75 g) unbleached all-purpose flour
½	teaspoon baking powder
½	teaspoon fine salt
1	cup (200 g) granulated sugar
½	cup (113 g) melted unsalted butter
2	large eggs
1	large egg yolk
1	teaspoon vanilla extract
½	teaspoon freshly grated lemon zest

WARM PEAR CARAMEL

⅔	cup (135 g) packed light or dark brown sugar
3	tablespoons cornstarch
2	cups (500 ml) pear nectar or apple cider
6	tablespoons (90 ml) heavy whipping cream
3	tablespoons unsalted butter
¼	teaspoon coarse kosher or sea salt

Preheat the oven to 375°F (190°C). Butter the inside of a 10-inch (25-cm) springform pan and set it aside.

Melt 1 tablespoon of the butter in a large skillet over medium-high heat and sauté the pears until they are softened, about 10 minutes. Remove the skillet from the heat and set it aside.

Sift the flour, baking powder, salt, and sugar into a large bowl. In a small bowl, whisk together the melted butter, eggs, egg yolk, vanilla, and lemon zest. With a wooden spoon, stir the wet ingredients into the dry ingredients and blend until smooth. With a wooden spoon, fold in the sautéed pears and their juices. Spoon the batter into the prepared pan and smooth the top with a spatula.

Bake for 30 to 35 minutes, or until the top of the cake is browned and a cake tester inserted in the center comes out clean. Remove the cake from the oven and let it cool in the pan for 30 minutes, then remove the sides of the pan and transfer the cake to a serving platter.

For the Warm Pear Caramel, whisk the brown sugar and cornstarch together in a large saucepan. Press out any lumps with your fingers. Stir in the nectar and cook the mixture over medium-high heat, whisking constantly, until large bubbles form around the perimeter of the pan and the sauce thickens, about 10 to 12 minutes. Remove the pan from the heat and whisk in the cream, butter, and salt.

Cut the cake into slices and serve each slice drizzled with the warm caramel.

Cane Syrup Gingerbread with Vanilla Baked Apricots

English, French, and German settlers all brought their different versions of gingerbread to American shores, so we've had a taste for spice cake from the earliest days. European gingerbread was usually sweetened with honey, but in America that changed to molasses, cane syrup, or even sorghum. I prefer to use pure cane syrup to make this gingerbread, as the syrup adds a slight spicy note of anise or licorice and is lighter in texture than molasses. This smooth, very gingery cake is delicious served with warm Vanilla Baked Apricots (page 58), which you can bake alongside the cake.

MAKES 1 (9-INCH/23-CM) SQUARE CAKE

½ cup (113 g) unsalted butter, at room temperature, plus more for the pan

½ cup (110 g) packed light brown sugar

½ teaspoon baking soda

2 large eggs

1½ cups (188 g) unbleached all-purpose flour

½ cup (125 ml) pure cane syrup, molasses, or sorghum

1 tablespoon ground ginger

½ teaspoon ground cinnamon

½ teaspoon ground allspice

1 teaspoon freshly grated lemon zest

½ cup (125 ml) buttermilk

1 recipe Vanilla Baked Apricots (page 58), prepared

Preheat the oven to 350°F (180°C). Butter a 9-inch (23-cm) square baking pan and set it aside.

In the bowl of an electric mixer, cream together the butter and brown sugar until light and fluffy, about 3 minutes. Add the baking soda and eggs and beat well to combine. The mixture will look curdled, but that will disappear. Beat in the flour and cane syrup, then add the ginger, cinnamon, allspice, and lemon zest. Finally, add the buttermilk and beat the mixture until it forms a smooth batter. Pour or spoon the batter into the prepared pan.

Bake for 30 minutes, or until a cake tester inserted in the center comes out clean and the sides of the cake have pulled away from the pan. Remove the cake from the oven and let it cool slightly before serving.

To serve, place squares of gingerbread on individual plates and top them with Vanilla Baked Apricots (page 58). Store the gingerbread, covered, at room temperature for up to 3 days.

Cranberry-Orange Cake with Warm Cranberry-Orange Caramel

In North America, the quintessential winter flavor pairing is cranberry and orange. When you serve this simple cake, snowy with confectioners' sugar, with a warm drizzle of caramel, you won't mind the cold.

MAKES 1 (9-INCH/23-CM) CAKE

CRANBERRY-ORANGE CAKE

2	cups (190 g) unbleached all-purpose flour
½	cup (100 g) granulated sugar
2	teaspoons baking powder
¼	teaspoon fine salt
1½	tablespoons unsalted butter, plus more for the pan
	Zest of 1 orange, about 2 teaspoons
12	ounces (375 g) fresh cranberries, cut in half
1	cup (250 ml) whole milk

CRANBERRY-ORANGE CARAMEL

½	cup (110 g) packed light brown sugar
½	cup (100 g) granulated sugar
1	teaspoon freshly grated orange zest
½	cup (125 ml) cranberry juice
¼	teaspoon fine salt
2	tablespoons unsalted butter
	Confectioners' sugar, for dusting

Preheat the oven to 350°F (180°C). Butter the inside of a 9-inch (23-cm) round cake pan. Line the cake pan with a round of parchment paper, and butter the paper. Set the pan aside.

Sift the flour, sugar, baking powder, and salt together into a large bowl. Cut in the butter with a pastry blender or two table knives until the mixture resembles small crumbs. With a wooden spoon, stir in the orange zest and cranberries, then the milk. The batter will be a little lumpy. Pour the batter into the prepared pan.

Bake for 45 minutes or until the cake is browned on top and the sides start to pull away from the pan. Remove the cake from the oven and let it cool in the pan for 30 minutes.

For the Cranberry-Orange Caramel, stir the sugars, orange zest, cranberry juice, and salt together in a medium saucepan over medium-high heat until the sugars dissolve. Bring the mixture to a boil, then remove the pan from the heat and stir in the butter until well blended. The caramel will thicken as it cools.

Invert the cake onto a serving plate and dust it with confectioners' sugar. To serve, cut the cake into slices and drizzle each portion with warm caramel. Store the cake, covered, at room temperature for up to 3 days.

Cranberry + Orange

Tart red cranberry and sunny orange are two flavor beacons that shine out when the skies are gray and a blizzard is howling. Cranberries, grown in bogs in New England and Wisconsin, are great keeping fruits, coming into season right before Thanksgiving. When the turn-of-the-century Christmas tree was strung with homemade paper and cranberry garlands, kids would also find an orange in the bottom of their stockings "hung by the chimney with care." So it's no wonder we've carried that festive association forward.

"The mingled scents of chocolate, vanilla, heated copper, and cinnamon are intoxicating, powerfully suggestive; the raw and earthy tang of the Americas, the hot and resinous perfume of the rain forest."

Joanne Harris, *Chocolat*

Almond Keeping Cake

When you've got a lot going on, being able to make a deliciously reliable dessert ahead of time brings a sigh of relief, along with another check-off on the to-do list. A keeping cake is one that does just that—keeps for days after you bake it. Moist and almond-scented, this golden brown cake can be highlighted with seasonal fruit like Skillet Cranberries (page 59), Vanilla Baked Apricots (page 58), strawberries in Rosy Strawberry Syrup (page 29), or Passion Fruit Blueberries (page 72). It can also go the chocolate route with Chocolate Ganache (page 27) or Hot Fudge Sauce (page 25).

MAKES 1 (10-INCH/25-CM) CAKE

1 cup plus 1 tablespoon (245 g) unsalted butter, at room temperature, divided

¼ teaspoon fine salt

1 cup (200 g) granulated sugar

8 ounces (250 g) almond paste, finely grated

½ teaspoon vanilla extract

½ teaspoon almond extract

5 large eggs

1 cup (82 g) sifted cake flour, plus more for the pan

½ teaspoon baking powder

Confectioners' sugar, for dusting the finished cake (optional)

Preheat oven to 325°F (160°C). Butter a 10-inch (25-cm) springform pan with 1 tablespoon of the butter and dust it with cake flour; tap out the excess over the sink.

In the bowl of an electric mixer, cream the remaining 1 cup of butter with the salt and sugar until creamy and light, about 5 minutes. Add the grated almond paste and beat for another 2 to 3 minutes on high speed until the mixture is almost white (the abrasiveness of the sugar granules helps to break down the almond paste). Turn the speed to low and add the vanilla and almond extracts, then the eggs, one at a time. Sift the cake flour and baking powder over the batter and fold it into the batter with a spatula until the batter is smooth and uniform in color. Pour the batter into the prepared pan and smooth the top.

Bake for 40 to 45 minutes or until the cake is golden brown and a cake tester inserted into the center comes out clean. Remove the cake from the oven and immediately release it from the pan onto a cooling rack to cool completely.

If desired, dust the finished cake with confectioners' sugar. To serve, cut the cake into slices. Store the cake, covered, at room temperature for up to 1 week.

Seersucker Lemon-Blueberry Cake Roll

During the holidays, some bakers like to make a pumpkin cake roll or the fancier bûche de Noël. But there is a lot to be said for a summery version, too, in stripes of pale yellow and deeper blue. With a blueberry-studded, lemon-scented filling, this cake has the fresh look and taste of summer. The cake roll is also easy to make, in stages, and to roll up. The cake itself is very supple, but the trick is to follow the timing exactly—7 minutes in the oven and 5 minutes to cool before spreading on the filling and rolling it up. Make this a polka dot cake, if you like, by piping dots instead of stripes. The only tricky part of this recipe is that the whole baking sheet needs to go in your freezer for 30 minutes for the stripes to set. Adapted from a recipe by Raiza Costa, who blogs at Dulce Delight.

MAKES 1 (11-INCH/28-CM) CAKE ROLL

LEMON-BLUEBERRY FILLING

1   (8-ounce/226-g) package cream cheese, at room temperature

3   tablespoons unsalted butter, at room temperature

1   cup (120 g) confectioners' sugar, sifted

2   teaspoons freshly grated lemon zest

1   pint (300 g) fresh blueberries

    Confectioners' sugar, for dusting

BLUEBERRY STRIPES

2   large egg whites

2   tablespoons granulated sugar

2   tablespoons unsalted butter, at room temperature

⅔   cup (75 g) unbleached all-purpose flour, plus more as needed

    Blue and black gel food coloring

LEMON CAKE

4   large egg whites

1   teaspoon cream of tartar

½   cup plus 1 tablespoon (112 g) granulated sugar, divided

4   large egg yolks

5   tablespoons (45 g) unsalted butter, melted

¾   cup (85 g) unbleached all-purpose flour

    Fresh blueberries for garnish

    Mint sprigs, for garnish

Line a 17 x 11-inch (43 x 28-cm) baking sheet with parchment paper, and set it aside.

For the Lemon-Blueberry Filling, place the cream cheese, butter, confectioners' sugar, and lemon zest in a food processor and process until the mixture is smooth and creamy. Set the filling aside.

Arrange a piece of parchment paper on a flat work surface and dust it with confectioners' sugar.

(recipe continues)

For the Blueberry Stripes, in a medium bowl, whisk together the egg whites, sugar, butter, and flour until smooth and thick. Color the batter with gel food coloring until you get a dark blue. Put the mixture in a squirt bottle with a ⅛ to ¼-inch (3 to 6-cm) opening at the tip. Squirt squiggly blueberry stripes, about 1 inch (2.5 cm) apart, across the short side and down the length of the prepared baking sheet. Transfer the baking sheet to the freezer and let the stripes set for 30 minutes.

When you're ready to bake the cake, preheat the oven to 400°F (200°C).

In the bowl of an electric mixer, beat the egg whites with the cream of tartar until foamy, about 2 minutes, then continue beating on medium speed until soft peaks form, about 2 minutes more. Add half of the sugar to the bowl, 1 tablespoon at a time, and beat on high speed until white, billowy peaks form, about 7 minutes total. Set the bowl aside.

In a medium mixing bowl, combine the egg yolks with the remaining 4 tablespoons of sugar, the melted butter, and the flour; whisk together until smooth. Add half of the beaten egg whites and fold them in with a spatula or large metal spoon until they are well incorporated. Add the rest of the beaten egg whites and continue folding them in until the batter is uniform in color.

Remove the baking sheet with the blueberry stripes from the freezer. Spoon the cake batter over the stripes in a thin layer. Smooth the batter with an offset spatula or flour scraper. Using your forefinger, make a clean channel along the perimeter of the cake batter so that the batter does not touch the sides of the pan.

Bake for 7 minutes or until the cake feels firm when you press it in the middle and the edges are just starting to turn golden.

Immediately remove the baking sheet from the oven and invert the cake onto the confectioners' sugar–dusted piece of parchment paper. Peel the parchment paper from the top of the cake and discard it. Place a new sheet of parchment paper over the cake. Holding the cake at both ends, carefully and quickly turn the cake over again and peel off the parchment so that the confectioners' sugar–dusted side is facing up. Let the cake cool for 5 minutes.

Spread the cake with the filling and sprinkle with the blueberries. Starting with a short side, carefully and firmly roll up the cake.

To serve, transfer the cake to a platter, cut it into slices, and set each slice on an individual plate with a scattering of blueberries and fresh mint sprigs. If necessary, trim the ends a little bit with a serrated or cake knife to make a more attractive cake roll.

"To lie under an acacia tree that last week and look up through the branches at its frail leaves and white flowers quivering against the blue of the sky while the least movement of the air shook down their scent, was a great happiness."

Elizabeth von Arnim, *The Enchanted April*

Chocolate Truffle Cake

One of the joys in my life is my culinary book club. Eight like-minded women who love food and cooking get together every month and bring a dish from the selected book. Over the years, we've shared births, deaths, divorces, marriages, adoptions, up-sizing, down-sizing, and all kinds of career triumphs and challenges. One balmy September night, we gathered at Liz Benson's house for a salute to Chocolat *by Joanne Harris. We dined on French food indoors and discussed the book. Then, as the movie screen flickered to life and the sun went down, we sat on her patio, not in Kansas anymore, but transported to the little town of Villeneuve where Vianne starts her story. We tucked into this truffle cake, sugar-crisp on the top, smooth and unctuous in the middle, mysterious with spices and dark chocolate. You can make the chocolate ganache up to 3 days ahead of time: just warm it before spreading on the gluten-free cake, which also keeps well at room temperature. Inspired by* Chocolat, *but adapted from a recipe in* Beyond Parsley, *by the Junior League of Kansas City, Missouri.*

MAKES 1 (8-INCH/20-CM) CAKE

8   ounces (250 g) dark or semisweet chocolate, cut into small pieces
1   cup (227 g) unsalted butter, at room temperature, cut into pieces, plus more for the pan
1½   cups (300 g) granulated sugar
5   large eggs
1   recipe Venezuelan Spiced Chocolate Ganache (page 27)

Preheat the oven to 350°F (180°C). Butter an 8-inch (20-cm) round cake pan, line the bottom with parchment paper, and then butter the parchment paper. Set the pan aside.

In a saucepan over medium heat, melt the chocolate and whisk until smooth. Whisk in the butter, a little at a time, until it has melted completely. Remove from the heat. Whisk in the sugar until smooth, then add the eggs and whisk vigorously by hand until the chocolate batter ribbons from the whisk, about 3 minutes.

Spoon the batter into the prepared pan and set the cake pan in a larger baking dish filled with hot water to reach halfway up the sides of the pan.

Bake for 90 minutes or until the cake starts to shrink from the sides of the pan. Remove the cake from the oven and let it cool for 1 hour in the pan. The cake will deflate slightly.

Cover the cake with plastic wrap or foil and chill it in the refrigerator until it has set, about 2 hours.

To serve, run a knife around the perimeter of the pan and invert the cake onto a cake plate. Spread the top and sides of the cake with the ganache. Or, if you like, set the container of ganache in a large bowl of hot water and stir until it melts and is pourable, then drizzle it over the cake before serving. Store the cake, covered, at room temperature for up to 1 week.

Citrus-Glazed Sweet Potato Bundt Cake

The "you're home now" flavor and silky texture of this dessert appeal to a wide audience. You can make the Orange-Cardamom Syrup for the glaze up to a week ahead of time. This keeping cake will see you through the holidays.

MAKES 1 (10-INCH/25-CM) BUNDT CAKE

Baking spray, for the pan

1 cup (227 g) unsalted butter, at room temperature

2 cups (500 g) granulated sugar

1 (16-ounce/454-g) can sweet potato purée, drained and mashed

1 teaspoon vanilla extract

5 large eggs

3 cups (285 g) cake flour

2 teaspoons baking powder

½ teaspoon baking soda

1 teaspoon ground cinnamon

¼ to ½ teaspoon freshly grated nutmeg

¼ teaspoon fine salt

1 recipe Orange-Cardamom Syrup (page 32)

Preheat the oven to 350°F (180°C). Spray a 10-inch (25-cm) Bundt cake pan with baking spray and set it aside.

In the bowl of an electric mixer, cream together the butter and sugar until light and fluffy, about 5 minutes. Add the sweet potatoes and vanilla and beat until well combined. Add the eggs, one at a time, mixing thoroughly after each addition.

In a medium mixing bowl, sift together the flour, baking powder, baking soda, cinnamon, nutmeg, and salt. Beat the flour mixture into the sweet potato mixture, 1 cup (250 ml) at a time, mixing well after each addition until the batter is smooth and uniform in color. Pour the batter into the prepared pan.

Bake for 60 to 75 minutes or until the cake is golden brown on top and a toothpick inserted near the center comes out clean. Remove the cake from the oven and let it cool completely in the pan on a wire rack for 30 minutes, then invert it onto a serving plate.

Just before serving, drizzle the glaze over the cooled cake so that it drips down the sides. Slice and serve. Store the cake, covered, at room temperature for up to 1 week.

Luscious Cream Cheese Pound Cake

Pound cake comes to the American dessert repertoire from European roots. The French call it "quatre quarts" or four-fourths. The British just knew that a pound of four different ingredients—butter, flour, eggs, and sugar—was needed to make this cake and named it accordingly. With three different flavorings creating a trio of taste, this moist and fragrant pound cake is wonderful served with fresh berries, Hot Fudge Sauce (page 25), or a warm Sea Salt Caramel (page 24). Leftovers can also make a wonderful bread pudding, baked in small loaf pans (page 197).

MAKES 1 LARGE TUBE OR BUNDT CAKE

1½ cups (179 g) unsalted butter, at room temperature, plus more for the pan

1 (8-ounce/226-g) package cream cheese, at room temperature

3 cups (603 g) granulated sugar

6 large eggs

3 cups (248 g) sifted cake flour, plus more for the pan

2 teaspoons vanilla extract

2 teaspoons almond extract

2 teaspoons brandy

Confectioners' sugar, for dusting

Preheat the oven to 325°F (160°C).

Butter and flour the inside of a 10-inch (3-L) tube or Bundt cake pan. Turn the pan upside down and tap out the excess flour over the sink; set the pan aside.

In the bowl of an electric mixer, cream together the butter and cream cheese until the mixture is smooth, about 4 minutes. Add the sugar and beat until it becomes light and fluffy. Add the eggs, one at a time, beating well after each addition. Beat in the flour, a little at a time, until well blended. Using a spatula or wooden spoon, stir in the vanilla, almond extract, and brandy. Pour the batter into the prepared pan and smooth the top.

Bake for 1 hour and 10 minutes, or until a toothpick inserted in the center comes out clean. Remove the cake from the oven and let it cool in the pan for 10 minutes, then invert the cake onto a cooling rack to cool completely.

Dust the cake with confectioners' sugar before serving. Store it, covered, at room temperature for up to 1 week.

VARIATIONS

THIS RECIPE CAN ALSO MAKE TWO 9 X 5-INCH (23 X 13-INCH) LOAVES, which take 45 minutes to bake, or four 5¾ x 3¼ x 2¼-inch (15 x 8 x 6-cm) mini loaves, which take 30 minutes to bake.

Rainbow Cake with Robin's Egg Blue Frosting

There's something about a rainbow cake that just makes you smile. A rainbow cake can be vivid or more pastel, which I prefer. Cake flour and sour cream in the batter ensure that your cake will be moist and tender, yet firm and sturdy—just what you want for a rainbow cake. If you like, you could stir about ½ teaspoon flavoring into each tinted batter—lemon zest for yellow, orange zest for orange, lime zest for green, and so on. This makes a festive birthday cake for any age.

MAKES ONE (8-INCH/20-CM) 4-LAYER CAKE

1½   cups (340 g) unsalted butter, at room temperature, plus more for the pans

3   cups (700 g) granulated sugar

3   large eggs, beaten

1½   cups (375 ml) non-fat plain Greek yogurt, or full-fat sour cream

1½   teaspoons vanilla extract or almond extract

3   cups (260 g) sifted cake flour

2   teaspoons baking powder

½   teaspoon fine salt

     Gel food coloring, as desired

1   recipe Swiss Meringue Buttercream Frosting (page 205), tinted robin's egg blue (with Wilton gel color Teal)

Preheat the oven to 350°F (180°C). Butter four 8-inch (20-cm) round cake pans and set them aside.

In the bowl of an electric mixer on low speed, cream together the butter and granulated sugar for 5 to 7 minutes until light and fluffy. Beat in the eggs, sour cream, and vanilla. Then beat in the flour, baking powder, and salt for 1 minute, scraping down the sides of the bowl.

Set out four small bowls. Spoon ¾ to 1 cup (about 453 grams) of the batter into each bowl and tint each with food coloring to your desired color, such as pale yellow, green, coral, and pink. Keep in mind that the color will somewhat darken and brown during baking. Spoon a bowl of tinted cake batter into each of the prepared pans and smooth the tops with a spatula or knife.

Bake for 25 to 28 minutes or until the cake comes away from the sides of the pan and is springy to the touch in the center. Remove the cakes from the oven and let them cool in the pan for 15 minutes, then invert them onto cooling racks to cool completely, about 30 minutes.

To assemble the cake, save the most domed layer for the top. Place the flattest layer on a serving plate and spread the top with ½ cup (125 ml) of the frosting. Place another layer on top and frost the top of that layer with another ½ cup (125 ml) of frosting. Place the third layer on top and frost it with another ½ cup (125 ml) of frosting. Place the last layer on top of the stack. Using an offset spatula, frost the sides of the cake with half of the remaining frosting, then use the rest for the top of the cake.

Slice and serve. Store the cake, covered, at room temperature for up to 3 days.

"American layer cake is a great invention and, if you consider the variations, as remarkable as jazz."

Delia Ephron, author, screenwriter, producer, and bakery-lover

Strawberry Birthday Cake

Made with an easy yet delicious one-bowl yellow cake, this birthday cake is the traditional American layer confection with a twist. Strawberry syrup colors as well as flavors the buttercream frosting, evoking lazy summer childhood days. You can also make a blueberry, raspberry, blackberry, or passion fruit version simply by using a different syrup and fruit for the filling. Add colored sprinkles to the top and sides, unfurl a homemade cake bunting across the top of the cake, and the kid in anyone will be happy.

MAKES ONE (8-INCH/20-CM) 3-LAYER CAKE

Baking spray, for the pans

3 cups (285 g) unbleached all-purpose flour, sifted

2 cups (500 g) granulated or raw sugar

1½ tablespoons baking powder

1½ teaspoons fine salt

¾ cup (170 g) unsalted butter, at room temperature

1½ cups (375 ml) whole milk

1½ teaspoons vanilla extract

3 large eggs

1 recipe Flavored Syrup Buttercream Frosting (page 24) made with Rosy Strawberry Syrup (page 29), prepared

1 pint (250 g) fresh strawberries, hulled and finely chopped

1 recipe Homemade Colored Sprinkles (page 35), prepared, for garnish (substitute store-bought decorations)

Preheat the oven to 350°F (180°C). Spray the inside of three 8-inch (20-cm) round cake pans with baking spray and set them aside.

Sift the flour, sugar, baking powder, and salt together into the bowl of an electric mixer. Add the butter, milk, and vanilla and beat on medium speed for 3 to 4 minutes, occasionally scraping down the sides of the bowl. Add the eggs and beat again at medium speed for 3 more minutes or until well blended. Divide the batter evenly among the prepared pans.

Bake for 25 to 28 minutes or until a toothpick inserted in the center of a cake comes out clean. Remove the cakes from the oven and let them cool in the pans for 10 minutes, then invert the cake layers onto cooling racks. Let the layers cool completely before assembling the cake.

To assemble the cake, save the most domed layer for the top. Place the flattest layer on a serving plate, spread the top with ½ cup (125 ml) of the frosting, and scatter it with half of the strawberries. Place another layer on top, frost with another ½ cup (125 ml) of frosting, and scatter with the remaining half of the strawberries. Place the third layer on top of the stack and frost the top of it with ½ cup (125 ml) of frosting. Using an offset spatula, frost the sides of the cake with half of the remaining frosting, then frost the top with the rest. Sprinkle colored sprinkles on the top and partially down the sides of the frosted cake.

Slice and serve. Store the cake, covered, at room temperature for up to 3 days.

French Bouquet Cake

The "Grandmother's Flower Garden" or "French Bouquet" quilt pattern features small hexagons, usually of pastel printed cottons, arranged in large geometric flower shapes. It offers endless possibilities for color combinations and the way the blocks can be set together, just as this cake does. My lemon-scented sour cream cake is topped with colorful garden confetti in this summer dessert. But use your own creativity to change the flavoring to orange or vanilla or almond, and the topping to whatever catches your fancy in the garden. I like to mix at least three different colors of edible flower blossoms and petals: lavender buds or bachelor's button petals, scented pink rose petals, and yellow pot marigold or coreopsis petals—all organic and unsprayed.

MAKES 1 (9-INCH/23-CM) CAKE

CAKE

12	fresh lemon verbena, lemon balm, or mint leaves
1	cup (227 g) unsalted butter, at room temperature, plus more for the pan
2	cups (500 g) granulated sugar
2	large eggs, beaten
1	(8-ounce/250-g) container sour cream or Greek yogurt, such as Fage
2	cups (165 g) sifted cake flour
1¼	teaspoons baking powder
¼	teaspoon fine salt
	Zest and juice of 1 lemon
1	teaspoon vanilla extract

FLOWER GARDEN CONFETTI

1	cup mixed fresh edible flower petals and blossoms
½	cup (125 ml) sanding or sparkle sugar

Preheat the oven to 350°F (180°C). Butter a 9-inch (23-cm) springform pan and press the verbena or mint leaves into the sides of the pan to make a pattern. Set the pan aside.

In the bowl of an electric mixer on low speed, cream the butter and granulated sugar for about 5 to 7 minutes or until light and fluffy. Beat in the eggs and sour cream, and then add the flour, baking powder, and salt and beat well to blend. Beat in the lemon zest, lemon juice, and vanilla until the batter is smooth and uniform in color.

Pour the batter into the prepared pan, being careful not to dislodge the herb leaves.

Bake for 50 to 60 minutes, or until a cake tester inserted in the center of the cake comes out clean. Remove the cake from the oven and let it cool in the pan for 30 minutes.

Remove the sides of the pan and invert the cake onto a serving plate or cake stand.

For the Flower Garden Confetti, gently mix the edible blossoms and petals with the sugar in a small bowl.

Sprinkle the confetti over the cake; slice and serve. This cake is best enjoyed the same day it is made.

Edible Flowers + Cakes

Edible flowers can add vivid or gentle color as well as flavor to all kinds of confections. Consider the peppery nasturtium, the fragrant rose petal, and pungent flowering herbs like rosemary (the flower tastes a bit spicier than the herb). Make sure that the flowers come from pesticide-free gardens or, even better, grow your own. (Note: Most edible flowers should be consumed in moderation.)

BASIL. Different varieties produce either bright white, pale pink, or soft lavender flowers.

BEE BALM. Also known as wild bergamot; the red flowers have a minty flavor.

BORAGE. The star-shaped flowers are a pretty cornflower blue and taste a bit like cucumber.

CHERVIL. This small white flower has a slight anise flavor.

FENNEL. Pretty yellow flowers have a mild anise taste.

SCENTED GERANIUM. The flower will taste like the variety, i.e., a lemon-scented geranium has a lemon-scented flower. Use the petals to garnish desserts and drinks.

LAVENDER. The pale to dark purple flowers have sweet citrusy floral notes.

MINT. The cone-shaped flowers are pretty snipped with a bit of the leaves for flavor and garnish in salads, desserts, and lamb dishes.

NASTURTIUM. The jewel-tone colors of this peppery flower are one of the happiest additions to salads and make gorgeous garnishes for savory or sweet dishes.

PANSY. The petals have a sweet, mild, grassy flavor.

ROSE. The flavors of roses range from strawberry to green apple depending on the variety.

ROSEMARY. The flower is a mild version of the leaf.

VIOLET. This also includes Johnny jump-ups and violas with colors of the rainbow from violet to yellow to pale peach and apricot.

"A party without cake is just a meeting."

Julia Child, food television pioneer and cookbook author

Vegan Devil's Food Cake with Coffee-Coconut Buttercream

It's the dawn of a new age of cake. Now, even traditional bakers need a really, really good vegan and gluten-free cake recipe in their repertoire because "you never know." Like the Chai Cupcakes (page 165), you'd never know this moist, one-bowl cake was vegan just by tasting it. The Coffee-Coconut Buttercream is equally fabulous. It doesn't taste like coconut at all, just rich and creamy. (Don't forget to chill the can of coconut milk for 24 hours before you make the buttercream. Now, I just keep a can in the refrigerator at all times.) This cake looks dramatic and delicious "naked," or not frosted on the sides. The billowy buttercream provides a contrast of color, flavor, and texture in the middle of the cake and mounded on top. Although this recipe makes a wonderful cake, it doesn't work well for cupcakes, as the batter sticks to the cupcake papers and doesn't rise as high.

MAKES ONE (9-INCH/23-CM) 2-LAYER CAKE

VEGAN DEVIL'S FOOD CAKE

1½   cups (188 g) unbleached all-purpose flour or gluten-free unbleached all-purpose flour blend

1   cup (200 g) raw sugar

1   cup (250 ml) real maple syrup, preferably Grade B

⅔   cup (42 g) unsweetened cocoa powder

1   teaspoon baking soda

1   teaspoon fine salt

2   cups (500 ml) brewed coffee or warm water

2   teaspoons vanilla extract

⅔   cup (150 ml) canola oil, plus more for the pans

2   teaspoons distilled white or apple cider vinegar

COFFEE-COCONUT BUTTERCREAM

1   (13.5-ounce/398-ml) can full-fat coconut milk or coconut cream, refrigerated for 24 hours

3   cups (360 g) confectioners' sugar, sifted

2   teaspoons vanilla extract

½   teaspoon espresso powder or instant coffee

TOPPING

Dairy-free chocolate sprinkles or 2 ounces (60 g) dairy-free dark chocolate bar, for garnish

(recipe continues)

Preheat the oven to 350°F (180°C). Oil the inside of two (9-inch/23-cm) round cake pans and set them aside.

In a large bowl, whisk together the flour, sugar, maple syrup, cocoa powder, baking soda, salt, coffee, vanilla, canola oil, and vinegar until smooth. Divide the batter evenly between the prepared pans.

Bake for 30 minutes, or until a toothpick inserted in the center of a cake comes out clean. Remove the cakes from the oven and let them cool in the pans on wire racks for 30 minutes, then loosen the sides of the cakes with a table knife and invert the cake layers onto the racks to cool completely.

For the Coffee-Coconut Buttercream, open one end of the coconut milk can and pour off the coconut water (reserve it for use in soups or drinks). Open the other end and scrape out the solidified coconut cream into the bowl of an electric mixer. If you are using coconut cream, simply spoon it out into the bowl. Add the confectioners' sugar and vanilla to the bowl and beat on low speed until blended, then turn the speed to high and whip the mixture until it is light and billowy, about 5 minutes total. Stir in the espresso powder with a rubber spatula.

To assemble the cake, place one cake layer on a cake plate. Spread the top of the layer with one-third of the frosting. Place the second layer on top and gently press down so the frosting reaches the edges of the bottom cake layer. Spoon and spread the remaining frosting on top of the cake.

For the topping, sprinkle the frosted cake with chocolate sprinkles or use a vegetable peeler to make curls of dairy-free dark chocolate. Slice and serve. Store the cake, covered, in the refrigerator for up to 3 days.

"Chocolate strolls up to the microphone and plays jazz at midnight, the low slow notes of a bass clarinet. Chocolate saunters down the runway, slouches in quaint boutiques; its style is je ne sais quoi. *Chocolate stays up late and gambles, likes roulette. Always bets on the noir."*

From "Ode to Chocolate" by Barbara Crooker

Over-the-Rainbow Cake

Sometimes using what we have grown, preserved, or simply have on hand brings a sense of well-being. Just imagine Auntie Em rummaging around in her Kansas farm kitchen, looking for ingredients to bake a cake. From what she grew in her garden, milked from her cows, gathered from her hens, or ground from her wheat, she could create this three-layer rainbow cake. The pale, natural colors come from puréed pickled beets, yellow summer squash, and mashed sweet potato, all smoothed over with a cloud of buttermilk frosting.

···· **MAKES ONE (8-INCH/20-CM) 3-LAYER CAKE** ····

OVER-THE-RAINBOW CAKE

½   cup (113 g) unsalted butter, at room temperature, plus more for the pans

1¼   cups (250 g) granulated or raw sugar

2   large eggs

1   cup (250 ml) buttermilk

2   teaspoons freshly grated lemon zest

1   cup (125 g) unbleached all-purpose flour, plus more for dusting the pans

1   cup (95 g) cake flour

1   tablespoon baking powder

1   teaspoon fine salt

⅓   cup (75 ml) pickled beets, puréed

⅓   cup (75 ml) finely grated yellow summer squash, from 1 medium

⅓   cup (75 ml) mashed, cooked sweet potato, from 1 medium

BUTTERMILK FROSTING

½   cup (113 g) unsalted butter, at room temperature

1   teaspoon freshly grated lemon zest

1   teaspoon vanilla extract

1   (16-ounce/454-g) package confectioners' sugar, sifted

4   to 5 tablespoons (50 to 65 ml) buttermilk

Preheat the oven to 350°F (180°C). Butter and flour the insides of three (8-inch/20-cm) round cake pans. Turn the pans upside down and tap out the excess flour over the sink; set the pans aside.

In the bowl of an electric mixer, cream together the butter and sugar on medium speed until the mixture is light-colored, about 5 to 7 minutes. Beat in the eggs, buttermilk, and lemon zest until well combined. Sift in the flours, baking powder, and salt and beat on low speed until the batter is smooth and uniform in color. Divide the batter among three bowls. With a fork, blend the puréed pickled beets into the first bowl, the grated squash into the second bowl, and the mashed sweet potato into the third bowl. Spoon the batter from each bowl into a prepared cake pan and smooth the tops with a spatula.

(recipe continues)

Bake for 18 to 22 minutes, or until a toothpick inserted in the center of a cake comes out clean. Remove the cakes from the oven and let them cool in the pans for 10 minutes, then run a table knife around the perimeter of each pan to loosen the sides of the cake, and invert the cakes onto wire racks to cool completely.

For the frosting, in the bowl of an electric mixer, cream together the butter, lemon zest, and vanilla on medium speed until smooth, about 4 minutes. Add the confectioners' sugar, one-third at a time, alternating with the buttermilk until you have a smooth frosting.

To assemble the cake, place one layer on a cake plate and spread the top thinly with frosting. Top with the second layer and spread the top of that layer thinly with frosting, then place the third layer on the top of the stack. With an offset spatula or a table knife, frost the sides of the cake, then the top with the frosting. Cut the cake into slices and serve. Store it, covered, at room temperature for up to 2 days.

Coffee-Walnut Blitz Torte

Just thinking about this cake brings back wonderful memories of happy birthdays as I was growing up. Maybe part of the delight is remembrance, but another part is the magical chemistry in the way all the elements of this confection work together. The crunchy meringue dusted with sugary spiced walnuts, the mellow cake, and the creamy coffee custard filling create a sum much greater than the parts. And the cake tastes even better the next day.

MAKES 8 TO 10 SERVINGS

Baking spray, for the pans

COFFEE-WALNUT BLITZ TORTE

1	cup (82 g) sifted cake flour
1	teaspoon baking powder
⅛	teaspoon fine salt
½	cup (113 g) unsalted butter, at room temperature
1¼	cups (255 g) granulated sugar, divided
4	large eggs, separated
1	teaspoon vanilla extract
3	tablespoons whole milk

TOPPING

½	cup (125 ml) chopped walnuts
1	tablespoon granulated sugar
½	teaspoon ground cinnamon
1	recipe Coffee Pastry Cream (page 23)

Preheat the oven to 350°F (180°C). Spray the inside of two (9-inch/23-cm) round cake pans with baking spray and set them aside.

For the Blitz Torte, sift the flour, baking powder, and salt together into a medium bowl; set the bowl aside. In the bowl of an electric mixer, cream the butter with ½ cup (100 g) of the sugar until creamy. Add the egg yolks and continue beating for several minutes until the mixture is pale and fluffy. Beat in the vanilla, milk, and sifted dry ingredients. Divide the mixture between the prepared cake pans. Wash the beaters and the batter bowl under hot running water and dry them well.

In the clean bowl of the electric mixer, whip the egg whites until they form stiff peaks, about 4 minutes. Gradually add the remaining ¾ cup (155 g) of sugar and beat until the meringue is glossy, about 7 minutes total. Spread half of the meringue over the cake batter in each pan. Combine the walnuts, sugar, and cinnamon in a small bowl, and sprinkle this mixture over the meringue.

Bake for 30 minutes, or until a knife inserted in the center of each cake comes out clean. Remove the cakes from the oven and let them cool completely in the pans.

To assemble the cake, remove the cakes from the pans and place one layer on a cake plate. Spread the pastry cream on the cake and place the second layer on top. Slice and serve. Store the cake, covered, at room temperature for up to 2 days.

Strawberry Shortcut Cake with Basil Whipped Cream

I have never been a big fan of biscuit-like shortcake, which either gets dry or soggy way too easily. When my sister Julie Fox sent me this shortcut cake recipe, adapted from one by Paul and Gina Neely, I was eager to try it. My sister was particularly pleased by how easy the spongy yellow cake was to cut in half and how delicious the strawberries were with it. A little hint of fresh basil in the whipped cream makes it all come together.

○ ·········· MAKES 1 (8-INCH/20-CM) CAKE ·········· ○

BASIL WHIPPED CREAM

- ¼ cup (30 g) packed fresh basil leaves
- 1 cup (250 ml) heavy whipping cream
- 3 tablespoons confectioners' sugar, sifted

SHORTCUT CAKE

- 1 cup (125 g) unbleached all-purpose flour, plus more for dusting the pan
- ¾ cup (160 g) granulated sugar
- 1 teaspoon baking powder
- ½ teaspoon fine salt
- 4 tablespoons (57 g) unsalted butter, melted, plus more for the pan
- 1 large egg, beaten
- ½ cup (125 ml) whole milk
- 1 teaspoon vanilla extract

ROSY STRAWBERRY FILLING

- 1 pound (500 g) fresh strawberries (reserve 5 berries for garnish)
- 1 recipe Rosy Strawberry Syrup (page 29) or Fresh Herb Syrup (page 30), prepared

GARNISH

Fresh basil or other herb leaves

For the Basil Whipped Cream, combine the basil leaves and cream in a medium saucepan over medium-high heat. Heat the cream until bubbles form around the perimeter of the pan, then remove the pan from the heat, cover it, and let the cream infuse for 30 minutes. Strain out the basil leaves and refrigerate the flavored cream until you are ready to assemble the cake.

Preheat the oven to 375°F (190°C).

Butter the bottom and sides of an 8-inch (20-cm) round cake pan. Line it with a parchment paper circle, butter the paper, and dust the pan with flour. Tap out the excess flour.

(recipe continues)

For the Shortcut Cake, in a medium bowl, whisk together the flour, sugar, baking powder, and salt, then whisk in the butter, egg, milk, and vanilla until almost smooth (there can be small lumps). Pour the batter into the prepared pan.

Bake for 22 to 25 minutes or until a toothpick inserted in the center of the cake comes out clean. Remove the cake from the oven and let it cool in the pan on a wire rack for 10 minutes. Using a knife, loosen the cake from the sides of the pan and invert it directly onto the wire rack to cool completely.

For the Rosy Strawberry Filling, set aside five strawberries for the garnish. Hull and finely chop the remaining strawberries. Heat the Rosy Strawberry Syrup in a medium saucepan over medium-high heat until it begins to bubble at the edges. Add the strawberries to the pan and cook, stirring, for 2 to 3 minutes or until the berries are slightly warm and glistening. Remove the pan from the heat and set it aside to cool for 10 minutes.

To assemble the cake, cut the cake in half horizontally, using a serrated knife. Begin to cut the cake in half until you reach the center of the cake, then turn it a quarter turn and keep cutting and turning until you reach your original cut mark. Use the knife to help separate the layers. Place the bottom layer, cut-side up, on a cake plate. Spread the layer with the strawberry mixture. Top with the remaining layer, cut-side down. Arrange the five reserved strawberries on top of the cake.

In the bowl of an electric mixer, whip the flavored cream with the confectioners' sugar until soft peaks form. Dollop the whipped cream on each slice of cake and garnish with fresh basil or other herb leaves.

Espresso-Chocolate Cheesecake

A good cheesecake helps you celebrate, mourn, ponder, or handle just about anything that life throws at you. When you need a strong shoulder to lean on, plus a take-charge push, then it's a chocolate and espresso cheesecake that's up to the job.

MAKE 1 (9-INCH/23-CM) CHEESECAKE

CHOCOLATE CRUST

- 1½ cups (198 g) chocolate wafer cookie or chocolate graham cracker crumbs
- ¼ cup (60 g) sliced almonds
- ½ cup (113 g) unsalted butter, melted

ESPRESSO-CHOCOLATE CHEESECAKE

- 2 (8-ounce/226-g) packages cream cheese, at room temperature
- 1¼ cups (250 g) granulated sugar
- 1 tablespoon instant espresso powder or instant coffee
- 1 cup (250 ml) sour cream
- 4 large eggs, beaten
- ½ cup (175 g) semisweet chocolate chips

GARNISH

- 1 cup (350 g) semisweet or white chocolate chips, melted
- ½ cup pomegranate seeds

Preheat the oven to 350°F (180°F).

For the Chocolate Crust, process together the cookie crumbs and almonds in a food processor until finely ground. Drizzle in the melted butter and pulse until the mixture is well blended. Pat the crust mixture onto the bottom and up the sides of a 9-inch (23-cm) springform pan; set the pan aside.

In the bowl of an electric mixer, beat the cream cheese until smooth, about 2 minutes. Add the sugar and espresso powder, beat well to combine, and then add the sour cream and eggs and beat the mixture until smooth. Using a rubber spatula, fold in the chocolate chips.

Pour the mixture into the prepared crust.

Bake for 30 to 35 minutes, or until a cake tester inserted in the center of the cake comes out clean. Turn the oven off, open the oven door, and let the cheesecake cool inside for 30 minutes before serving.

To garnish, drizzle with melted chocolate and sprinkle with pomegranate seeds. Slice and serve. Cover and store it in the refrigerator for up to 3 days.

INDEX

Note: Page references in *italics* indicate photographs.